# THE MODERN WORLD

# THE MODERN WORLD

## A POLITICAL STUDY SYLLABUS

YUSUF MEHERALLY

GYAN

*Published by*

Gyan Publishing House
5, Ansari Road
Daryaganj, New Delhi-110002
Phone: 011-47034999, 9811692060
E-mail: books@gyanbooks.com

*Distribution Network*
gyanbooks.com
India, USA, Canada, UK, Australia



ISBN: 978-93-7225-111-1 (PB)

First Published, 1945

2nd Impression 2025

*Printed at:* Gyan Press, Delhi.



**THE MODERN WORLD: A POLITICAL STUDY SYLLABUS**
Author: YUSUF MEHERALLY

# THE MODERN WORLD

## A POLITICAL STUDY SYLLABUS

BY

**YUSUF MEHERALLY**

PADMA PUBLICATIONS LTD
BOMBAY

To

**ASOKA MEHTA**

**Most generous of friends**

*BY THE SAME WRITER*

LEADERS OF INDIA (5th Edition)
A TRIP TO PAKISTAN (2nd Edition)

## CONTENTS

PREFACE

### Part I

Countries & their Peoples

INTERNATIONAL AFFAIRS ... ... 9

**ASIA**

INDIA : ... ... 14

Background Books ... ... 16

The Rise of the Nationalist Movement ... ... 18

Recent Political Developments ... 19 and 180

Constitutional History ... ... 20

The Communal Problem ... 21 and 180

Pakistan ... ... 21

The Indian States and Their People ... ... 21

Economic Conditions ... 22 and 181

Cultural Heritage ... ... 25

Books For Further Study ... ... 26

Mahatma Gandhi ... ... 28

Biographical Note ... 29 and 181

Of Literary Interest ... 31 and 181

CHINA ... ... 34

JAPAN ... ... 40

THE FAR EAST :

Burma—Ceylon—"Dutch" East Indies—"French" Indo-China—Korea—"British" Malaya, Manchuria, Mongolia, Tibet Thailand ... 44 and 181-2

THE ARAB WORLD :

ARABIA AND YEMEN ... 48 and 183

EGYPT (See under Africa) ... ... 49

IRAQ ... ... 49

PALESTINE & TRANSJORDAN ... ... 50

SYRIA AND LEBANON ... 51 and 183

IRAN ... 51

AFGHANISTAN 52 and 183

## EUROPE:


ENGLAND ... ... 3
FRANCE ... ... 58
GERMANY ... ... 62
ITALY ... ... 66
SCANDINAVIA ... ... 69
SOVIET RUSSIA ... ... 72
SPAIN ... ... 78
TURKEY ... ... 80
OTHER EUROPEAN COUNTRIES:
AUSTRIA—BALKAN COUNTRIES—BELGIUM—CZECHO-SLOVAKIA—EIRE—HOLLAND—HUNGARY—POLAND—PORTUGAL—SWITZERLAND 84 and 183


## AMERICA:


THE UNITED STATES OF AMERICA .. .. 89
THE NEGRO IN AMERICA ... 93 and 183


### SOUTH AMERICA:


ARGENTINE 96
BRAZIL 97
CHILE 97
MEXICO, etc. 98

CANADA ... ... 98


## AFRICA:


99
BACKGROUND BOOKS
ABYSSINIA
EGYPT
NORTH AFRICA
EAST AFRICA
WEST AFRICA
SOUTH AFRICA, etc.
SUDAN, MOROCCO, etc. ... ... 183


## AUSTRALASIA:


AUSTRALIA 103
NEW ZEALAND 104

## PART II

### SOCIAL AND POLITICAL TRENDS

SOCIALISM .. ... 104

HISTORY OF SOCIALISM 104 and 183
THEORY OF SOCIALISM ... ... 106
MARX AND ENGELS ... ... 107
UTOPIAN SOCIALISM ... ... 109
FABIAN SOCIALISM ... ... 110
SYNDICALISM ... ... 110
ANARCHISM ... ... 111
GUILD SOCIALISM ... ... 112
SINGLE TAX ... 112 and 184
COMMUNISM ... ... 113
TROTSKYISM ... ... 114
MANAGERIAL REVOLUTION ... ... 114
THE INTERNATIONALS ... ... 115

CAPITALISM

THE CASE FOR CAPITALISM 117 and 184
EVOLUTION OF CAPITALISM ... ... 117
FINANCE CAPITALISM ... ... 118
TRUSTS AND CARTELS ... 119 and 184
POVERTY AND PLENTY ... ... 119
THE NEW DEAL ... ... 119
CAPITALISM AND WAR ... ... 120
CAPITALISM AND PLANNING ... ... 121
CAPITALISM AND DEMOCRACY ... ... 122

FASCISM ... ... 124

IMPERIALISM ... ... 126

NATIONALISM ... ... 129

PEACE & WAR

PEACEFUL CHANGE ... ... 131
WAR—IN THEORY AND PRACTICE ... ... 132
THE LEAGUE OF NATIONS ... ... 133
MANDATES, PLEBESCITES, SANCTIONS, LEND-LEASE... 134
WORLD RE-ORGANISATION ... ... 134

**THE LABOUR MOVEMENT**

BACKGROUND BOOKS ... 136 and 184

Reference, European Labour—Labour History—I. L. O. General Strikes—Unemployment—Social Security—Eastern Industrialisation

TRADE UNIONISM ... ... 139

Theory and Practice of Trae Unionism, History, Documents

COUNTRY BY COUNTRY ... 141 and 184

Africa — China — England — France — Germany — India — Italy — Japan — New Zealand — Sweden — Soviet Russia — U. S. A.

**THE PEASANT MOVEMENT**

BACKGROUND BOOKS ... ... 149

Rural Economics—World Agriculture—Village Communities—Industry and Rural Life

COUNTRY BY COUNTRY ... ... 150

China, Denmark, England, Germany, India, Italy, Japan, Mexico, Soviet Russia, Sweden, U. S. A.

**THE WOMEN'S MOVEMENT**

BACKGROUND BOOKS ... ... 157

From Subjection To Comradeship—Fight For Rights—Women And Revolution

COUNTRY BY COUNTRY ... ... 158

China, England, France, Germany, India, Japan, The Near And The Middle East, Soviet Russia, Turkey, U. S. A.

**THE YOUTH MOVEMENT**

COUNTRY BY COUNTRY ... ... 162

England, China, Germany, India, Italy, The Near And Middle East, Soviet Russia, U. S. A.

**THE CO-OPERATIVE MOVEMENT**

BACKGROUND BOOKS 167 and 184

World Co-operation—Progress and Reaction—Co-operative Organisation and Reconstruction—Agricultural Co-operation

COUNTRY BY COUNTRY ... ... 169

China, France, Germany, Italy, Great Britain, India, Japan, Scandinavia, Soviet Union, U. S. A. and The Americas

**OTHER SUBJECTS** 172

Political Science—Economics—Sociology—Anthropology—Philosophy—Science—Art—Miscellaneous

REFERENCE BOOKS ... ... 177

SOME REFERENCE BOOKS ON INDIA ... ... 179

**ADDITIONAL NAMES** 180

# PREFACE

The momentous events of the past few years have greatly quickened the consciousness of mankind. They have also stimulated a vast curiosity, a yearning to know and to understand the modern world in all its complexities. In India, faced with the question of winning her freedom, the desire, if anything, is even more pronounced and widespread. This little book is written in the hope that it may in a small way help the reader to meet this need, to understand the world around himself.

I have called it a Political Study Syllabus, because it deals mainly wih international affairs, political and social theory and the great progressive movements that are seeking to reshape the world. But it will be seen that quite a number of allied subjects are also touched upon. At least some of the more important books of cultural, literary and sociological interest are included, as also those on economic history. In several cases Biographical Notes and Literary Footnotes have been added. As far as I know there is no book in the English language, printed in India or abroad, that conforms to this plan or furnishes all the information, in an easily classifiable form, as will be found here. The section on India is naturally bigger than that of other countries, but for this I need make no apology.

Some years ago in a book entitled *What To Read* I had made a similar effort. It received a welcome beyond my expectations, both from the press and the public. The edition was sold out in a very short time and it has been out of print since. From many letters I have been able to gather, that it had been of use not only to individual readers but also to study circles, libraries and to booksellers, and the demand for it has persisted. The present effort is not a revision of my earlier book. but rather a new book, with a number of new sections and features, and over twice its size. A wearying and prolonged illness, with its enforced leisure, has alone made it possible to complete it.

The Syllabus has been divided into two parts. The first deals with international affairs and in it will be found material on the various countries of the world. The second part is concerned with political and social theory, Capitalism, Socialism, and other 'isms' and 'wasms'. A consideration of the Labour, Peasant, Women's Youth and Co-operative Movements follows next. Finally there is a section on *Other Subjects* giving essential background books on social sciences and one on important Books of Reference.

The books have been chosen with great care and I have naturally striven to select only the best. Differing standpoints are invariably represented, as they should be in a study syllabus. Since books on Labour, Peasant, Women's and Youth movements are given separately, they are not included in their respective countries over again, in order to save space. A detailed Contents will, I hope, facilitate easy reference.

YUSUF MEHERALLY

# INTERNATIONAL AFFAIRS

OUTLINE OF HISTORY by H. G. Wells, (Cassell), 8/6, pp. 1242.

The first and still the finest history of the world in one volume. Its publication has revolutionised the writing of history. The same writer's *Short History of the World* is available in the Penguin Books, 9d.

GLIMPSES OF WORLD HISTORY by Jawaharlal Nehru, (Lindsay Drummond), 10/6, pp. 993, (1939).

A fascinating glimpse into world history. Written in the shape of letters to his daughter, during a number of prison terms. Comparable to Wells' *Outline of History*. Contains 50 interesting maps by J. F. Horrabin.

OUR ORIENTAL HERITAGE by Will Durant, (Simon & Schuster) $5, pp. 1052, 5th Pr. 1942.

A truly inspiring book by the author of *The Story of Philosophy*. In its exciting pages is given the history of Egyptian civilisation in the Near East to the death of Alexander, and of India, China and Japan from ancient times to the present day. Also a brilliant essay on 'The Nature and Foundations of Civilisation.' Reading it is a liberal education.

PAGEANT OF ASIA by Kenneth Saunders, (Oxford), 7/6, pp. 452, (1934).

A study of the three civilisations of India, China and Japan from their earliest beginnings.

CONTEMPORARY INTERNATIONAL POLITICS by W. R. Sharp & Grayson Kirk, (Farrar & Rinehart), $3.50, pp. 840, (1940).

An attempt to examine the forces responsible for the motivation of foreign policies. The authors employ 'a functional interpretation of the interlocking of geography, population, race, nationalism, technology, economics and government,' method-of-analysis, to the more conventional method.

A HISTORY OF EUROPE by H. A. L. Fisher, (Arnold), 14/-, pp. 1301, (1936). Reprinted 1943.

An ambitious history of Europe by one of the most noted of modern historians.

A SHORT HISTORY OF INTERNATIONAL AFFAIRS by G. M. Gathorne Hardy, (Oxford), Royal Inst. of Int. Affairs, 12/6, pp. 514, 3rd. Ed. 1942.

A scholarly study of international affairs from the founding of the League of Nations to the outbreak of the Second World War. Remarkable to say, India is not mentioned in the whole book even once.

EUROPE ON THE EVE—THE CRISIS OF DIPLOMACY by F. L. Schumann, (Robert Hale), 18/-, pp. 600, Revised 1943.

NIGHT OVER EUROPE—THE DIPLOMACY OF NEMESIS by F. L. Schumann, (Robert Hale), 18/-, pp. 636, 1941.

A study of international cross-currents during the six years from the rise of Hitler to the Second World War (1933-1939). A trenchant examination of the foreign policies of England, France, Germany and Italy, and to a lesser extent of the other European countries. *Night Over Europe* is a sequel and continues the story from 1939 to the spring of 1941, with the same mastery of detail and erudition.

INSIDE EUROPE by John Gunther, (Hamish Hamilton), 12/6, pp. 527, 1936, Revised 1940.

INSIDE ASIA by John Gunther, (Hamish Hamilton), 12/6, pp. 659, 1939, Revised 1942.

INSIDE LATIN AMERICA by John Gunther, (Hamish Hamilton), 12/6, pp. 388, 1943.

The finest one volume survey of contemporary European, Asian and South American affairs in English.

They also contain inimitable pen pictures of the leading personalities of Europe, Asia and Central and South America. *Inside Europe* is by far the best of the three.

THE MIRROR OF THE PAST: LET IT REFLECT THE FUTURE by K. Zilliacus, ("Vigilantes"), (Gollancz) 7/6, pp. 286, 1944.

A brilliant study of international anarchy, imperialism and power politics and the connection between them and the capitalist economic system, with a surprising wealth of quotation. The lessons of the bitter past are reviewed as a guide to the problems of the future.

---

## ADDITIONAL REFERENCES

---

STUDY OF HISTORY by A. J. Toynbee, (Oxford), 6 Vols., Vols. 1 to 3 £2-12-6, pp. 1518, Vols. 4 to 6 £3-10, pp. 2070. (1940).

ECONOMIC HISTORY OF EUROPE by S. B. Clough & C. B. Cole, (D. C. Heath, Boston) $4, pp. 841, 1941.

INTERNATIONAL POLITICS by F. L. Schumann, (MacGraw Hill), $5, pp. 733, Revised 1941.

FIFTY YEARS OF EUROPE by J. A. Spender, (Cassell) 7/6, pp. 436, 1936.

THE TWENTY YEARS' TRUCE: (1919-1939) by Robert M. Rayner, (Longmans), 12/6, 1943.

WORLD POLITICS: (1918-1936) by R. Palme Dutt, (Gollancz), 5/-, pp. 382, 1936.

OUR OWN TIMES: (1913-1934), A Political and Economic Survey by S. King-Hall, (Nicholson & Watson), 12/6, 1935.

REFLECTIONS ON THE REVOLUTION OF OUR TIME by H. J. Laski, (Allen & Unwin) 15/-, 1944.

A HISTORY OF NATIONALISM IN THE EAST by Hans Kohn, (Routledge), 25/-, pp. 476, 1929.

NATIONALISM AND IMPERIALISM IN THE HITHER EAST by Hans Kohn, (Routledge), 15/-, pp. 339, 1929 Revised 1942.

ISLAM TO-DAY by A. J. Arbery and Rom Londau, (Faber), 12/6, pp. 258, 1943.

SPEECHES AND DOCUMENTS ON INTERNATIONAL AFFAIRS: (1918-1937), Edited by A. Berridale Keith, (Oxford), World's Classics, 2 Vols. 3/-, each, pp. 346 & 278, 1938.

HISTORY OF MILITARISM by Alfred Vagts, (Allen & Unwin), 18/-, pp. 510, 1938, 33 Illustrations.

A STUDY OF WAR by Quincy Wright, (Cambridge University Pr.), 2 Vols., £4-10, 1943.

THE WAR IN OUTLINE (1914-1918) by Captain Liddel Hart (Modern Library), 95 cents, pp. 285, 1936. Revised 1939.

BATTLE FOR THE WORLD by Max Werner, (Gollancz), 7/6, pp. 288, 1941.

GLORY AND BONDAGE by Edgar Snow, (Gollancz), 10/6, pp. 263, 1945. (Thackers: Bombay). Rs. 7/8.

CONDITIONS OF PEACE by E. H. Carr, (Macmillan), 12/6, 1942.

THE ECONOMIC LESSONS OF THE NINETEEN-THIRTIES: A Report by H. W. Arndt, (Royal Inst. of Int. Affairs), 12/6, pp. 314, 1944.

# FOREIGN CORRESPONDENTS

The emergence of a new institution in international politics—the Foreign Correspondent, has been one of the notable developments of the past two decades. The credit for this must, in a large measure, go to the U.S.A. There are some hundreds of Foreign Correspondents on the track of news, in every part of the world, whereas at the turn of the century there were but a handful. Their efforts have resulted in a remarkable popularisation of contemporary political and social history. A few among them have made outstanding contributions. A much larger number have produced bright, racy and highly readable reports of their experiences. It is no easy task to pick and choose from the vast array of books in this field. Absolutely the two best are *Men and Politics* by Louis Fischer and *Days of Our Years* by Pierre van Paasen. Others like *Insanity Fair* by Douglas Reed, *In Search of History* by Vincent Sheean, and *Way of A Transgressor* by Negley Farson stand in a class by themselves. *Front Page Europe* by Denis Weaver *Journey Among Warriors* by Eve Curie, *Epitaph For Europe* by Paul Tabori, and *Brave Men* by Ernie Pyle are vividly written chronicles. Other books by Douglas Reed (*Disgrace Abounding, All Our Tomorrows* etc.,), Pierre van Passen (*This Day Alone*), Vincent Sheean (*Between the Thunder and the Sun*), Negley Farson (*A Transgressor in the Tropics*), make most interesting reading. Besides there quite a number of the more important reports on particular countries, will be found listed in appropriate places in the syllabus.

---

# ASIA

## INDIA

### BACKGROUND BOOKS

OUR INDIA by Minoo Masani (Oxford), Re. 1/-, & Rs. 3/12, pp. 166, 1940, 6th Ed., 1944.
The best introductory volume on India. A remarkable picture of the country as she is and as she might be. A distinguished book with 100 captivating illustrations. "I hail with delight the little book. It is about the one book I know which the man-in-the-street, who has neither love of learning nor love of country, would willingly read and find himself at the end of the reading, both a learned man and a usefully patriotic citizen." (*Indian Finance*).

THE PROBLEM OF INDIA by K. S. Shelvanker, (Penguin) 9d., pp. 254, 1940.
Interesting, informative and compact. Describes the historical background, the social and economic conditions of the people, British "interests" in India, the rise of the nationalist movement and the political crisis following World War II.

THE COMMUNAL TRIANGLE IN INDIA by Asoka Mehta & Achyut Patwardhan (Kitabistan, Allahabad) Rs. 4-8, pp. 263, 2nd Edition, 1942.
One of the two or three most important books on Indian politics published in recent years. A brilliant survey of the communal problem in its triangular setting. To call the problem 'Hindu-Muslim', as is usually done, the authors argue, is wrong for the Bri-

tish Government has played a great and often a decisive part in Hindu-Muslim relations. The first study to make an examination of the question, not only from the political, but also from the sociological and psychological angles. A wealth of documentation.

AUTOBIOGRAPHY by M. K. Gandhi, (Navjivan Publishing House, (Allahabad), Rs. 4/8, (1927-29).
The autobiography of one acclaimed as the greatest living man in the world. A document of unique interest. In its frankness comparable to Rousseau, in language strongly reminiscent of the Bible.

AN AUTOBIOGRAPHY: WITH MUSINGS ON RECENT EVENTS IN INDIA by Jawaharlal Nehru. (Lane), 7/6, pp. 623, 1936, 16th Reprint, 1942.
An epoch-making book. Written in prison, it is not only the autobiography of one of India's most distinguished leaders, but a political testament of incomparable importance. Required reading. The latest edition includes a supplementary chapter entitled 'Five Years Later'.

RISE AND FULFILMENT OF BRITISH RULE IN INDIA by Edward Thompson & G. T. Garrat (Macmillan) 21/-, 1934.
The best one-volume history of British rule in India, from its earliest beginnings under the East India Company. An exposure of British misdeeds, documented from British sources. The earlier portion is done brilliantly, but as they approach the present, the critical attitude of the authors becomes subdued, and they see in the abortive Round Table Conferences the 'fulfilment' of British Rule. Written with courage and sincerity and in a style that makes reading a pleasure.

MODERN ISLAM IN INDIA by W. Cantwell Smith (Minerva, Lahore), Rs. 10/-, 1943.
An examination of the social and political tendencies in present-day Islam in India. Packed with stimulating analysis and comment. A work of real merit and scholarship. The author, an American professor

at Lahore, has put students of the subject under a deep debt of obligation.

MODERN INDIA AND THE WEST Edited by L. S. S. O'Malley (Oxford), 36/-, pp. 834, 1941.

'A study of the Interaction of Their Civilisations' (Sub-title). An important study, sponsored by the Royal Int. of International Affairs, seeking to measure mainly the influence that the civilisation of the West has had on the life and thought of India, written by a group of English and Indian writers.

NOTE:—*Introduction to India* by F. R. Moraes & R. Stimson, (Oxford), Rs. 1/8, pp. 170, 1942 is a pleasant introductory volume, mainly intended for non-Indian readers.

## THE RISE OF THE NATIONALIST MOVEMENT

HISTORY OF THE INDIAN NATIONAL CONGRESS by Dr. Pattabhi Sitaramayya (All-India Congress Committee, Allahabad), Rs. 2/8, pp. 1038+104 1935.

The history of the first fifty years of the Congress from 1885 to 1935, published on the occasion of its Golden Jubilee. A scholarly work by a well known Congress leader, almost encyclopaedic in scope. Introduction by Babu Rajendra Prasad.

RENASCENT INDIA by H.C.E. Zacharias, (Allen & Unwin), 10/6, pp. 304, 1933.

The course of the Indian national movement from Raja Ram Mohan Roy to Gandhi, told in a sparkling and sympathetic style. The first section is devoted to the Social Reform Movement and the next three to the Political Movement. One of the best books on the subject.

HOW INDIA WROUGHT FOR FREEDOM: 1885-1914 by Annie Besant, (Theosophical Publishing House, Adyar, Madras) Rs. 3/-, pp. 710, 1915.

INDIAN NATIONAL EVOLUTION: 1885-1914 by Ambika Charan Mazumdar, (G. A. Nateson & Co., Madras) Rs. 3/-, pp. 519, 1915.

INDIA'S STRUGGLE FOR FREEDOM: 1919-1936 by Sardar Sardul Singh Caveeshar (National Publications, Lahore) Rs. 3/14, pp. 480, 2nd Edition 1936.

RISE AND GROWTH OF THE CONGRESS: 1885-1919 by C. F. Andrews & Girija Mukerji (Allen & Unwin) 7/6, 1938.

The story of India's fight for freedom by a group of well-known writers. Mrs. Besant's book written with passionate eloquence, contains a valuable historical introduction.

THE CRIPPS MISSION by R. Coupland, (Oxford), 12 annas, 1942.

THE MYSTERY OF SIR STAFFORD CRIPPS by Dr. Ram Manohar Lohia, (Padma Publications, Bombay) Annas 12/-, pp. 71, 1942.

Professor Coupland states the British case, Dr. Lohia gives a brilliant and effective reply.

INDIA UNRECONCILED (Hindustan Times Press, Delhi) Rs. 3/-, pp. 487, 1943.

CONGRESS RESPONSIBILITY FOR DISTURBANCES: 1942-1943 (Govt. of India, Delhi) annas 2/-, pp. 86, 1943.

GANDHIJI'S CORRESPONDENCE WITH GOVERNMENT: 1942-44 (Navjivan), Rs. 2/8, pp. 308, 1945.

Record of the stirring days of Quit India Movement of 1942-1943 and the stern actions of the Government

NOTE:—For further study see: *Nationalism & Reform in India* by W. Roy Smith (1938) a valuable study; *Young India* (1927) and *Unhappy India* (1928) both by Lala Lajpatrai; *Indian National Congress* by V. S. Srinivasa Sastri (1911), *India's Struggle for Swaraj* by R. G. Pradhan (1930), *Rise and Growth of Indian Nationalism* by M. A. Buch, 2 vols. (1939 & 1940). *Congress Rule in India* by Horace Alexander, (1938). For pro-British accounts. *Indian Unrest* and *India Old and New* both by Sir Valentine Chirol; *History of the Indian Nationalist Movement* by Sir Verney Lovett (1920).

Two books of very great interest are *The Indian Struggle* by Subhas Chandra Bose (1934) and *India Since the Mutiny* by Sir C. Y. Chintamani (1937).

## RECENT POLITICAL DEVELOPMENTS

A WEEK WITH GANDHI by Louis Fischer, (Indian Ed., International Book House, Bombay), Rs. 3/-, pp. 122, 1944, 15 Illustrations.

Brilliantly depicts the temper of India on the eve of the Quit India Movement in 1942. Louis Fischer, spent a week at Sevagram and the record of his conversations with Gandhiji on a variety of important subjects are faithfully recorded in this vivid document.

SUBJECT INDIA by H. N. Brailsford, (Gollancz), 6/-, pp. 223, 1943.

The conclusions of an internationally famous writer, on the 'relationship of estrangement' between imperialist Britain and subject India.

BEGGAR MY NEIGHBOUR by Lionel Fieldon, (International Book House, Bombay), Rs. 3/-, pp. 99, 1943.

An eloquent plea for immediate freedom for India, by the former Director of the All India Radio, in which the author has plenty of home-truths for his countrymen.

THE SIMLA TRIANGLE by Asoka Mehta and Kusum Nair (Padma Publications), Re. 1/-, pp. 82, 1945.

The Wavell Plan and its aftermath. The exciting journey to Simla, three years after the Rebellion of 1942. A narration of facts and a survey of developments.

Among recent books sympathetic to India's aspirations may be mentioned: *Revolution in India* by Francis Gunther, *India Since Cripps* by Horace Alexander, (Penguin), *India in Crisis* by J. S. Hoyland and *Strangers in India* by Panderal Moon. Among earlier books *The Present Condition of India* by L. M. Schiff (1939) and *India and Democracy* by Sir G. Schuster & G.

Wynt (1941), *Enlist India For Freedom* by Edward Thompson, (1941), *The People of India* by Kumar Ghoshal (1944) and *Salute To India* by W. Z. Hodge (1944), deserve special mention.

Two other valuable studies, which are also very good background books, are *India To-day* by R. Palme Dutt and *India: An American View* by Kate L. Mitchell.

## CONSTITUTIONAL HISTORY

THE INDIAN CONSTITUTIONAL PROBLEM by R. Coupland, (Oxford), Rs. 10/-, pp. 792, 1944.

A scholarly and comprehensive survey of India's constitutional problem, mainly from the pro-British angle, by the Beit Professor of Colonial History at Oxford. The first part covers the period from the Charter Act in 1833 to the Government of India Act 1935; the second describes political developments from 1936-1942 to the starting of the Quit India movement and includes a review of the work of the Congress ministries. In the final section the author suggests the lines along which the future constitution can be built. A creditable piece of research.

LANDMARKS IN INDIAN CONSTITUTIONAL AND NATIONAL DEVELOPMENT: 1600-1919 by Professor Gurumukh Nihal Singh (Indian Book Shop, Benares), Rs. 10/-, pp. 710, 1933.

A critical and penetrating study of constitutional development in India from the beginning of British rule, and a scholarly survey of the complex social, economic and administrative factors that have gone to the making of modern India. An analysis of the growth of the nationalist movement and of the steps taken by the British during three centuries of domination to circumscribe it. A book of exceptional interest, indispensable to every student of Indian affairs.

CONSTITUTIONAL HISTORY OF INDIA by A. Berridale Keith (Methuen) 16/-, pp. 581, 1936, 2nd Ed. 1937.

THE WORKING CONSTITUTION OF INDIA by S. M. Bose (Oxford), Rs. 20/-, pp. 716, 3rd Edition 1944.

INDIA'S CONSTITUTION AT WORK by C. Y. Chintamani & M. R. Masani, (Allied Publishers, Bombay), Rs. 3/12.

INDIAN CONSTITUTIONAL DOCUMENTS 2 Vols. Edited by A. Berridale Keith (Oxford), World's Classics, 3/-, each.

## THE COMMUNAL PROBLEM

*The Communal Triangle in India* and *Modern Islam In India,* both described above, are the two best books on the subject. Other good studies include:

THE INDIAN MUSSALMANS: Are They Bound In Duty To Rebel Against the Queen? by Sir William Hunter, (very rare). 1871.

THE PROBLEM OF MINORITIES IN INDIA by Dr. K. B. Krishna, (Allen & Unwin), 15/-, 1939.

THE PROBLEM OF MINORITIES by Dr. Dhiren Sen (Calcutta University Pr.) Rs. 7/-, 1940.

HINDUS AND MUSSALMANS IN INDIA by Atulananda Chakrabarty, (Thacker, Spink, Calcutta) 1940.

MUSLIM POLITICS by Humayun Kabir, (Rahman, Gupta & Rahman, Calcutta), Re. 1/-, 1943.

THE INDIA CHARTER by J. F. Kotewal, (Pub. by the author, Karachi), Rs. 10/8, pp. 459, 1944.

THE FRONTIER SPEAKS by Mohomed Yunus, (Minerva, Lahore), Rs. 6/-, pp. 248, 1942.

*For the viewpoint of the Muslim League consult*:

MUSLIM INDIA: RISE AND GROWTH OF THE ALL-INDIA MUSLIM LEAGUE by Mohomed Noman, (Kitabistan) Rs. 4/8, pp. 433, 1942.

RECENT SPEECHES AND WRITNGS OF MR. JINNAH (Mohomed Ashraf, Lahore) Rs. 6/-, pp. 506, 3rd Edition 1943.

INDIA'S PROBLEM OF HER FUTURE CONSTITUTION (Symposium) with a Foreword by M. A. Jinnah, Re. 1/-, 1940.

MUSLIM NATIONALISM IN INDIA by Muslim Study Circle, Bombay Rs. 2/8, 1942.

*The Hindu Mahasabha's angle is reflected in*

HISTORY OF THE HINDU MAHASABHA by Indra Prakash, Rs. 2/-.

WHIRLWIND PROPAGANDA OF V. D. SAVARKAR Edited and Published by Bhide Guruji, Rs. 3/-, pp. 676, 1941.

## PAKISTAN

Among a number of books on the subject published in recent years, the following are the more important:

PAKISTAN OR THE PARTITION OF INDIA by Dr. B. R. Ambedkar, (Thackers), Rs. 15/12, pp. 481, 1945, Maps. (First Ed. called *Thoughts On Pakistan*).

PAKISTAN by Dr. Rajendra Prasad, (Allied Publishers, Bombay) Annas 6/-, pp. 62, 1940.

THE PAKISTAN ISSUE by Nawab Nazir Yar Jung (Ashraf, Lahore), Rs. 3/12, 1943.

WHY PAKISTAN AND WHY NOT? by Professor K. T. Shah, (Pratibha Publications, Bombay) Rs. 5/-, pp. 284, 1944.

PAKISTAN by Dr. Shaukat Ansari, (Minerva Book Shop, Lahore), Rs. 3/8, pp. 130, 1944.

## THE INDIAN STATES & THEIR PEOPLE

The awakening among the people of the States has been one of the most important developments in India in recent years. The united resources of the Indian Princes and the British Government have been repeatedly needed to keep the agitation in check. These books throw light on the various facets of the States question.

INDIAN PRINCES UNDER BRITISH PROTECTION by P. L. Chudgar, 7/6, 1929.

INDIAN STATES AND GOVERNMENT OF INDIA by K. M. Pannikar, (Martin Hopkinson), 2nd Edition 1932.

UNITY IN FREEDOM: THE PROBLEM OF THE STATES by Purshotam Tricamdas, (Congress Socialist Party, Bombay) Annas 4/-, pp. 16, 1939.

THE UNITY OF INDIA by Jawaharlal Nehru, (Lindsay Drummond) Rs. 5/-, pp. 432, 1942.
(For Text of Presidential Address to the A. I. States Peoples Conference, etc.)

TO THE PRINCES AND THEIR PEOPLE by Mahatma Gandhi (Hingorani, Karachi), Rs. 5/8, 1942.

STATUS OF INDIAN PRINCES by Pyarelal.(Navjivan, Ahmedabad) Annas 4/-.

INDIAN STATES by K. R. R. Sastry, (Kitabistan), Rs. 2/8, pp. 236, 1941.

INDIAN STATES by K. M. Pannikar, (Oxford Pamphlet), Annas 6/-, 1942.

REPORT OF THE INDIAN STATES COMMITTEE, (Butler Committee), 1929.

BRITISH CROWN AND THE INDIAN STATES by The Standing Committee of the Chamber of Princes, 1929.

MEMORANDUM OF THE INDIAN STATES PEOPLES CONFERENCE TO THE BUTLER COMMITTEE, 1929.

## ECONOMIC CONDITIONS

### (a) GENERAL ECONOMIC SURVEYS

Among a number of general economic surveys *Indian Economics* by Professors Jathar & Beri, 2 Vols., *Our Economic Problem* by Profs. P. A. Wadia & K. T. Merchant (1943), *A Study of Indian Economics* by Prof. Pramathnath Bannerji (Reprinted 1944), *Indian Economics* by

Professors Malani & Soni (1936), *Indian Economic Life, Past and Present* by Prof. Brij Narain (1929), *Economic Development of India* by Vera Anstey (1929), *Economic Conditions in India* by Dr. P. P. Pillai (1925), and *Wealth of India* by Profs. P. A. Wadia & G. N. Joshi (1925) need to be singled out for special mention. A symposium to which a number of economists contribute, *Economic Problems of Modern India* Edited by Prof. Radhakamal Mukerji, 2 Vols. (Vol. 2 edited with Dr. H. L. Dey), is also of great interest. *The Economic Background* by Prof. K. T. Shah and others is a useful Oxford pamphlet (1942).

## (b) ECONOMIC HISTORY

For Indian economic history Romesh Chandra Dutt's *India Under Early British Rule* (1902) and *India Under the Victorian Age* (1904) rank as classics and are required reading. *Industrial Evolution in India* by D. R. Gadgil (2nd Ed. 1943) very ably covers the period from the fifties of the past century.

## (c) FINANCIAL HISTORY

Two excellent books on financial history are *Sixty Years of Indian Finance* by Prof. K. T. Shah (Popular Book Depot, Bombay) Rs. 10/-, pp. 460, 1921 (with supplement upto 1935), and *Financial Developments in Modern India*: 1860-1924 by Prof. C. N. Vakil. Both urgently need to be brought up-to-date.

## (d) SPECIAL STUDIES

Among special studies, of which there are a large number, the outstandnig are: *Poverty and Un-British Rule in India* by Dadabhoy Naoroji (1901), *Essays in Indian Economics* by M. G. Ranade, (1898), *India's Teeming Millions* by Gyanchand (1939), *Development of Capitalist Enterprise in India* by G. D. Buchanan (1934), *Problem of the Rupee* by Dr. B. R. Ambedkar, (1923), *Industrial Organisation in India* by Dr. P. S. Lokanathan, (1935), *The Structural Basis of Indian Economy* by H. Venkatasubbiah, *Indian Industrial Problems*, Edited by Dr. L. C. Jain (1942), *Heights of Simla* and *India Comes of Age* by Asoka Mehta (1937), and *The National Income of British India*: (1931-32), by Dr. V. K. R. V. Rao, *India's Rural Problem* by Sir Manilal Nanavati & Prof. J. J. Anjaria (1944). *India In Figures* by Dr. Ram Manohar Lohia (1941), *The Standard of Living* by M. L. Dantwala, (1945).

## (e) PLANNING

The National Planning Committee was set up in 1938 by Mr. Subhas Chandra Bose, then President of the Indian National Congress. Pandit Jawaharlal Nehru became its life and soul and he as President and Prof. K. T. Shah as Honorary General Secretary did meritorious work. The political crisis brought about a break in its activities, but most useful spade-work has been done. The publication of *A Plan For The Economic Development of India* by eight leading industrialists, (New Book Co., Bombay) 2 parts Re. 1/-, each, popularly known as the Tata-Birla Plan, and envisaging an expenditure of Rs. 10,000/- crores in 15 years, has stimulated fresh interest in the subject. Other plans have followed suit, and much interesting criticism. Among them may be mentioned *The Peoples Plan*, issued by M. N. Roy (Indian Federation of Labour, Delhi) Re. 1/-, 1944, *Planning For India* by Bimal C. Ghose, *A Plan For India* by Principal M. R. Shenoy. *The Gandhian Plan* by Principal S. N. Agarwal (Padma Publications) Rs. 2/8, purports to give Gandhiji's ideas on the economic development of India, and has been the focal point of much stimulating discussion.

## (f) IMPACT OF THE WAR ON INDIA

For the impact of World War II on India consult: *The Falling Rupee* and *The Financial Burden of the War on India* by Prof. C. N. Vakil, *War and Indian Economic Policy* by D. R. Gadgil, and *How India Pays for the War* by K. T. Shah, *War and Indian Economy* by V. K. R. V. Rao. For the effects of the war of 1914-1918 see: *Economic Consequences of the War for India* by Dr. S. G. Panandikar.

## CULTURAL HERITAGE

HISTORY OF ARYAN RULE IN INDIA: FROM THE EARLIEST TIMES TO THE DEATH OF AKBAR by E. B. Havell (Harrap), 12/6, pp. 583, 33 pages of Illustrations.

A remarkable book by a remarkable Englishman, who by his great scholarship and deep insight into Indian culture has done much to atone for the misdeeds of his countrymen in India. 'Havell Hall' at Tagore's Santiniketan commemorates the memory of one, who worked unceasingly to interpret India to the world. Some of his other books are *Ideals of Indian Art, A Handbook of Indian Art, Indian Sculpture and Painting,* and *The Himalayas in Indian Art.*

THE HINDU VIEW OF LIFE by Sir S. Radhakrishnan (Allen & Unwin), 3/6.

One of those books that casts a spell on the reader. Brilliant and lively, it prepares one for the same author's monumental *History of Indian Philosophy* in 2 Volumes.

INFLUENCE OF ISLAM ON INDIAN CULTURE by Dr. Tara Chand, (Hindustan Academy: Allahabad), Rs. 10/-.

A valuable study that shows the contribution of Islamic culture to the cultural synthesis of India.

A CULTURAL HISTORY OF INDIA DURING THE BRITISH PERIOD by A. Yusuf Ali (Taraporewala, Bombay), Rs. 10/-, 1940.

A pioneering study that breaks much fresh ground and is at the same time a work of great scholarship. Fills in a much-needed gap.

For other important studies see: *Our Oriental Heritage* by Will Durant; *Hindu Polity* by K. P. Jayaswal, *Ancient India* by A. J. Rapson, *India, What Can It Teach Us* by F. Max Muller; *Ancient India and South Indian History and Culture* by Dr. S. K. Aiyengar, *History of Indian and Indonesian Art* by Dr. A. K. Coomaraswamy,

*Indian Painting and Sculpture* by K. J. Khandalawala, *Cultural Heritage of India* Edited by Ramanand Chatterji, 3 Vols. *Modern Indian Culture* by Prof. D. P. Mukherji.

---

## FOR FURTHER STUDY

---

CAMBRIDGE HISTORY OF INDIA (Cambridge Univ. Pr.) 6 Vols.

CAMBRIDGE SHORTER HISTORY OF INDIA Edited by H. H. Dodwell (Cambridge Univ. Pr.) 18/-, pp. 970, 1934, Reprinted 1943.

OXFORD HISTORY OF INDIA by Vincent Smith (Oxford) 14/-, pp. 840, 1919. Several Reprints.

INDIA by Rene Grousset ('Civilisation of the East', Vol. 2), (Hamish Hamilton), 25/-, 1934.

WHITE SAHIBS IN INDIA by Reginald Reynolds, (Secker & Warburg), 12/6, pp. 440, 1937.

HISTORY OF THE NABOBS by Lester Hutchinson, (Allen & Unwin), 7/6.

RISE OF THE CHRISTIAN POWER IN INDIA by Major B. D. Basu, (R. Chatterji, Calcutta), Rs. 15/-, pp. 1011, 2nd Edition 1931.

INDIA UNDER THE BRITISH CROWN by Major B. D. Basu, (R. Chatterji, Calcutta), Rs. 10/-, pp. 570, 1933, 53 Illustrations.

HISTORY OF THE INDIAN MUTINY by Sir John Kaye and Col. G. B. Malleson, 6 Vols., 1888.

THE OTHER SIDE OF THE MEDAL by Edward Thompson, (Allen & Unwin), 5/-.

CREATIVE INDIA by Benoy Kumar Sarkar, (B. G. Paul) Rs. 15/-.

MARX & ENGELS ON INDIA (Kitabistan), Rs. 2/4, 1940.

PEOPLE OF INDIA by Sir Herbert Risley, (W. Thacker London), 1915.

CASTE AND RACE IN INDIA by G. S. Ghurye, (Allen & Unwin), 12/6, 1932.

CHANGING INDIA Edited by Raja Rao & Iqbal Singh (Allen & Unwin), 3/6, pp. 271, 1939.

THE INDIAN PRESS: A HISTORY OF THE GROWTH OF PUBLIC OPINION IN INDIA by Margarita Barnes (Allen & Unwin), 21/-, 1940.

THE INDIAN CIVIL SERVICE by Sir Edward Blunt (Faber) 6/-, pp. 292, 1937.

SOCIAL SERVICE IN INDIA Edited by Sir Edward Blunt (H. M. Stationery Office, London) 10/6, 1938.

INDIA AND THE WORLD by Jawaharlal Nehru (Allen & Unwin), 5/-, pp. 262, 1936.

UNITY OF INDIA by Jawaharlal Nehru (Lindsay Drummond) Rs. 5/-, pp. 432, 1941, (2nd. Ed.)

CONSTITUENT ASSEMBLY FOR INDIA by Dr. N. N. Gangulee (Allen & Unwin) 16/-, 1942.

INDIAN DIARY by E. S. Montagu (Heinemann) 21/-, pp. 410, 1930.

INDIAN LIBERALISM: (1918-1943), by V. N. Naik, (Padma Publications), Rs. 5/8, pp. 353, 1945.

INDIA ANALYSED Edited by B.P.L. & Freida Bedi, (Gollancz) 4 vols., 5/-, each, 1933-35.

INDIAN INDIA by N. Awab Zada, (Quality Press, London), 6/-, pp. 179, 1940.

HISTORY OF THE ARYA SAMAJ by Lala Lajpat Rai (Kapur: Lahore), Rs. 3/-, Reprinted 1932.

BRITISH IMPERIALISM IN INDIA by Joan Beauchamp (Martin Lawrence) 5/-, pp. 224, 1934.

GANDHI VERSUS THE EMPIRE by Dr. H. T. Mazumdar, New York, $2.00, 1933.

MY INDIA, MY AMERICA by Dr. K. Shridharani, (International Book House: Bombay), Rs. 7/12, pp. 479. In. Ed. 1945).

A TRIP TO PAKISTAN by Yusuf Meherally, (Padma Publications) Rs. 4/8, pp. 135. (1944).

WARNING TO THE WEST by Dr. K. Shridharani (International Book House, Bombay), Rs. 4/14, pp. 189, 1944.

A REPORT TO GANDHIJI by K. A. Abbas & N. G. Jog (Hind Kitabs, Bombay), Rs. 2/-, pp. 78, 1944.

CHURCHILL'S BLIND SPOT: INDIA by N. G. Jog, (New Book Co., Bombay), Rs. 5/-, pp. 228, 1944.

CRY OF DISTRESS: Bengal Famine, Edited by K. Santhanam, (Hindustan Times Pr.) Delhi, Rs. 2/-, 1943.

101 CARTOONS by Shankar, (Hindustan Times: Delhi), Rs. 5/-, 1937.

DEFENCE OF INDIA by Capt. G. V. Modak (Gwalior), Rs. 10/-.

THE ARMIES OF INDIA by Sir V. Lovell and Sir G. Macmunn.

## MAHATMA GANDHI

Easily the best thing on Gandhiji is the volume of diverse studies on himself presented to him on his 75th birthday. It is gorgeously produced and brilliantly edited by D. G. Tendulkar, M. Chalapathi Rau, Mridula Sarabhai, and Vithalbhai K. Jhaveri (Karnatak Publishing Co.,) Rs. 25/-, pp. 502, 1944, and beautifully illustrated. On his 70th birthday another volume, edited by Sir S. Radhakrishnan, *Mahatma Gandhi: Essays & Reflections on His Life and Work* had been published. Curiously enough, Romain Rolland's little book *Mahatma Gandhi* is still the best life. Gandhi's autobiography has already been listed above. The three volumes by C. F. Andrews are extremely readable: *Mahatma Gandhi's Ideas* (1929), *Mahatma Gandhi: His Own Story* (1930), *Mahatma Gandhi at Work* (1931) all published by Allen & Unwin. *Speeches and Writings of Mahatma Gandhi* edited by G. A. Nateson, is a marvel of inexpensive bookmaking.

His own writings, published by the Navjivan Press, Ahmedabad, show the amazing versatility of his interests. Special mention may be made of ***Hind Swaraj, Satyagraha in South Africa, Economics of Khadi,*** *Non-violence in*

*Peace and War, The States Problem* and *Christian Missions.* In the Gandhi series are the following: *To the Women, To the Students, Hindus & Muslims, To the Princes and Their People,* and *The Language Problem,* (Hingorani, Karachi).

The number of books seeking to interpret him are numerous. Mention may be made of *The Gandhian Way* by Acharya J. B. Kripalani, (Vora) *Gandhi and Gandhism* by Dr. Pattabhi Sitaramayya, (Kitabistan), 2 vols., *Studies in Gandhism* by Nirmal Kumar Bose, *War Without Violence* by Dr. K. Shridharani (Gollancz), *Gandhiji and the Congress Socialist Party* by Jai Prakash Narain, (C.S.P.) and *Independent India and A New World Order* by Y. G. Krishnamurti (Popular Book Depot, Bombay). *Power of Non-Violence* by Gregg, *Practical Non-Violence* and *Gandhi Vichar Dohan* (in Gujerati) by Mashruwala, *Gandhism* by P. Spratt, and *Gandhi* by Carl Heath.

Also *Socialism Reconsidered* by M. R. Masani, *Gandhism Reconsidered* by Professor M. L. Dantwala, both Padma Publications, *Is Gandhi A Socialist?* by M. R. Masani (Essay in 75th Gandhi Birthday Volume), *An Essay on Gandhian Economics* by Professor J. J. Anjaria (Vora) and *Economics of Non-Violence* by V. L. Mehta, (Hindustan Hamara Publications).

For Mrs. Gandhi, see *Sati Kasturba* by R. K. Prabhu (Hind Kitabs) *Kasturba Gandhi* by Rezaul Karim, (Chakrabarty Chatterji, Calcutta), and *Kasturba Gandhi* by Thomas (Orient Illustrated Weekly, Calcutta).

## *BIOGRAPHICAL NOTE*

For Jawaharlal Nehru apart from his fascinating *Autobiography* see *Nehru: The Rising Star of India* by Dr. Anup Singh. Another delightful book, *With No Regrets* by Krishna Hutheesingh, is a saga of the Nehru family.

*Maulana Abul Kalam Azad, Vir Vallabhbhai* (in Gujerati) and *Two Servants of God* (Khan Abdul Gaffar Khan and Dr. Khan Saheb) all by Mahadeva Desai and *Indian Struggle* by Subhas Bose are other works of great interest.

The best sketch of Mr. M. A. Jinnah is still Mrs. Sarojini Naidu's written in 1920 as an Introduction to his *Speeches and Writings*. Also see ***Eminent Mussalmans*** and *My Leader* by Z. A. Suleri.

Two books on Mr. V. D. Savarkar, Hindu Mahasabha leader are by Chitra Gupta and by J. S. Karandikkar, the latter in Marathi.

*Letters of Srinivasa Sastry* edited by T. N. Jagadisan and *Memories And Reflections* by Sir Chimanlal Setalvad give us glimpses into the thoughts of two eminent leaders of the Liberal Federation.

For stalwarts of an earlier generation consult: ***Dadabhai Naoroji*** by Sir R. P. Masani is based on a quarter century of research. It is probably the best volume of biography, written by an Indian writer so far, but it just falls short of doing full justice to the radicalism of the Grand Old Man of India. ***Sir Pherozshah Mehta*** by Sir H. P. Mody, ***Gokhale*** by Srinivas Sastry. ***Tilak*** by N. C. Kelkar (in Marathi) 3 vols. Only one volume of this important work has been translated into English. ***Bankim, Dayanand & Tilak*** by Aurobindo Ghosh, *A Nation In The Making* by Sir Surendra Nath Bannerji, *My Life: A Fragment* by Maulana Mohomed Ali, *Life of C. R. Das* by P. C. Roy, *J. N. Tata* by F. R. Harris are other well-known studies.

*Raja Ram Mohan Roy* by S. D. Collett, though written many years ago, is still the best short book on the Father of Indian Nationalism. Much interesting material will be found in the *Ram Mohan Centenary Volume*, edited by Ramanand Chatterji, especially the notes of Mr. Amal Home. Mr. Brajendra Nath Bannerji's numerous articles on the Raja, published over a number of years in the famous Calcutta Journal, ***Modern Review***, deserve a more permanent form.

*Sir Syed Ahmed Khan* by Col. Graham Smith (1909) is a sympathetic life of the founder of Aligarh. A far better one is *Hayat-e-Javid*, by the great poet Hali (in Urdu).

*Ramakrishna* and *Vivekananda* both by Romain Rolland and the *Autobiography* of Maharshi Debendra Nath Tagore are documents of unique interest.

Of those brave English friends who made the cause of Indian freedom their own, *A. O. Hume* by Sir William Wedderburn, *Annie Besant* by Geoffrey West, *Annie Besant* by Sri Prakash. *The Man Who Loved India* (C. F. Andrews) by J. S. Hoyland are available.

For the life of the most popular British Viceroy to India see *Lord Ripon* by Lucien Wolf and for one of the least popular, *Curzon* by Lord Ronaldshay. Studies of several of the earlier British Satraps—from *Clive* and *Warren Hastings* to *Canning* and *Dalhousie* will be found in the Rulers of India Series edited by Sir William Hunter.

The Publishing House of Natesan, Madras has rendered great service in publishing the speeches and writings of a number of our national leaders in uniform and inexpensive editions (generally Rs. 3/-, each, also various biographical studies in the volumes: *Eminent Mussalmans, Famous Parsis, Indian Christians, Famous Statesmen,* etc.

For biographical sketches of present-day leaders see *Men and Supermen of Hindustan* by Joachim Alva (Thackers, Bombay), Rs. 11/-, *Great Men of India* Edited by L. F. Rushbrook Williams (Times of India Pr.) Rs. 5/8, *Indian Testament* by Ela Sen, (Allen & Unwin) 7/6, and *Leaders of India* by Yusuf Meherally (Padma Publications) Annas 12/-.

---

## OF LITERARY INTEREST

---

### TAGORE

Much of the greatest literature of India is not still available in English translations. Fortunately, enough of Tagore is there to give an idea of his incomparable genius and versatility: *Gitanjali, Gardener, Crescent Moon* etc., (poems); *Chitra, Post-Office* (plays); *Chitra Lipi* (paintings); *Religion of Man* (philosophy); *Reminiscenes, Boyhood Days* (autobiography); *Hungry Stones* (short stories); *Gora, The Wreck, Home and the World* (novels). Latest to be available is *Farewell, My Friend,* translated by Krishna Kripalani and published in the

Pujah number of the 'Hindustan Standard', Calcutta 1944. *The Golden Book of Tagore* edited by Ramanand Chatterji, a book of worldwide appreciation, was presented to him on his 70th birthday. Of equal interest are the special Tagore numbers of the *Vishwa Bharati* Quarterly and of the *Calcutta Municipal Gazette,* both hard to obtain.

## IQBAL

Very little of Iqbal is available in English. *Reconstruction of Religious Thought in Islam, Secrets of the Self,* (Asrar-e-Khudi), and *Complaint and Answer* (Shikhwah and Jawab-i-Shikhwah) is about all. The last is very well translated by Altaf Hussain (Mohmed Ashraf, Lahore) Rs. 2/-, from whom more may be legitimately expected. For books on Iqbal see: *Iqbal: His Art And Thought* by Syed Abdul Vahid, *Iqbal As A Thinker* by a number of scholars, *Iqbal's Educational Philosophy* by K. G. Saiyedain, a very valuable study and *Metaphysics of Iqbal* by Dr. Ishrat Hasan, (all Mohomed Ashraf: Lahore). Also *Ruh-i-Iqbal* by Dr. Yusuf Husain Khan (in Urdu).

## AUROBINDO GHOSH

On Aurobindo Ghosh much has been written in recent years. His own books: *Collected Poems and Plays, Life Divine, Essays On The Gita* and *Renaissance In India* are known all over the world. The famous Indian musician, Dilip Kumar Roy has recorded his conversations with Sri Aurobindo and also with Rolland, Gandhi, Russell and Tagore in *Among The Great,* (N. M. Tripathi: Bombay).

## PROVINCIAL LITERATURES

The Indian P.E.N., under the Editorship of Madame Sophia Wadia has rendered a distinct service in sponsoring a series of books on provincial literatures in this country. Those on Assamese, Indo-Anglian, Telegu and Bengali literatures are out. The last by Anada Sankar and Lila Ray is of outstanding interest. (International Book House: Bombay).

There is a crying need for translations of the writings of Prem Chand and Sarat Chandra Chatterji. The latter's

*The Deliverance* has been translated by Dillip Kumar Roy (N. M. Tripathi, Bombay). Also *Sarat Chandra Chatterji* by Prof. Humayun Kabir (Padma) and *Prem Chand* by Madan Gopal may be consulted. A collected edition of Mrs. Sarojini Naidu's charming poems is *The Sceptred Flute* (Kitabistan) Fifteen volumes of poems and plays of Harindranath Chattopadhyaya are also available.

## ANTHOLOGIES

Four volumes of Anthologies of Poems, Essays etc. by Indian writers in English are being published. *The Peacock Lute,* (Anthology of Poems), *The Moving Finger,* (of critical essays) *The Earthen Bowl* (of short stories) and *The Blazing Shrine* (of plays). They are being edited by Prof. V. N. Bhushan (Padma Publications).

## FICTION

Among books of fiction written in English the following take a place: *Kanthapura* by Raja Rao, *A Passage to India* by E. M. Forster (Penguin), *An Indian Day* by Edward Thompson (Penguin), *Tomorrow Is Ours* by K. Ahmed Abbas, *The Coolie* by Mulk Raj Anand (Penguin), *We Never Die* by D. F. Karaka, *The Rains Came* by Louis Bromfield, *Hindu Holiday* by Eckersley (Penguin), and *Twilight in Delhi* by Ahmed Ali. *Best Stories of Modern Bengal* and *Tales of Rural Bengal* are two enjoyable anthologies of short stories.

## SOME CLASSICS

Among the classics *Ramayana and Mahabharata* translated in verse by R. C. Dutt (Everyman's Library), *The Song Celestial* and *The Light of Asia* both by Sir Edwin Arnold (Kitabistan) annas 12/- each, and *Shakuntala & Other Plays of Kalidas* (Everyman's Library) have secured a place in world literature.

# CHINA

## INTRODUCTORY

MODERN CHINA by Tan Yun-Shan (Kitabistan), Rs. 2/4, pp. 122, 2nd Ed., 1944.

A short history dealing with political changes, economic development and social progress of modern China. The author, an eminent scholar, is head of the Department of Chinese Studies at Shantiniketan.

IN WAR TORN CHINA by Kamaladevi, (Padma Publications) Annas 12, pp. 74, 1942. Third Ed., 1944.

An eye-witness account of war-torn China, written in a lively and chatty style, by one of the outstanding leaders of India's struggle for freedom. Chapters: In War-torn China, Nanking, Chunking, Economic Front, Army, Schools, Women, Cultural Progress.

MY COUNTRY AND MY PEOPLE by Lin Yu-Tang, (Heinemann), 7/6, pp. 363, 1936, 1943.

Pearl Buck in the preface calls this 'The truest, the most profound, the most complete, the most important book yet written about China.'

DESTINATION CHUNGKING by Han Suiyan, (Cape), 10/6, 1942.

The autobiography of a modern Chinese girl, who returns with a London degree and plunges straight into the fight for her country's freedom. A moving picture of China facing invasion and its terrors. A true mirror of the manifold sacrifices of China's youth.

## FOR FURTHER READING

A SHORT HISTORY OF CHINESE CIVILISATION by Tsui Chi, (Gollancz), 12/6, pp. 335, 1942.

A history of Chinese civilisation from the dawn of history to the present times. A brilliant piece of scholarship and research.

THE PROBLEM OF CHINA by Bertrand Russell, (Allen & Unwin), 7/6, 1922, Revised 1929.

The most outstanding book on China written by a non-Chinese. Bertrand Russell, who was for a year Professor of Philosophy at Peking, provides a penetrating account of the impact of the West on the ancient Chinese civilisation and the background of her present international relations.

THE VIGIL OF A NATION by Lin Yu-Tang, (John Day), $2.75, 1944 Illustrated.

CHINA LOOKS FORWARD by Sun Fo (Allen & Unwin), 12/6, 1944.

CHINA TAKES HER PLACE by Carl Crow, (Harper), $2.75, 1944.

A group of extremely interesting books interpreting battle-scarred China. Her effort under Marshal Chiang Kai-Shek in resisting invasion, the New Life Movement, opening up the country and its modernisation, are sympathetically reviewed.

CHINA THEN AND NOW by Jean Escarra, (Henry Vetch, Peking), $17.50 Chinese (Rs. 8/12), pp. 290, 1940.

An eminent French scholar, 20 years connected with China, writes about her people, geographical background, historical development, and great civilisation. Next, about her social, political, and technical reconstruction and finally, about Sino-Foreign relations.

THROUGH CHINA'S WALL by Graham Peck, (Collins). 12/6, pp. 318, 1941. Excellent Illustrations.
A travel book that is different and is much more than a mere travel book. 'A first rate book of its kind, ruthless, cool, humourous, uncluttered with personal feelings, but full of comprehension of the people.' (Pearl Buck).

CHINA AND JAPAN (Royal Inst. of Int. Affairs), 3/6,
A lucid, factual account of the relations of the two countries and their differences, put in a proper historical setting.

CHINA—AFTER SEVEN YEARS OF WAR, (China Pub. Co., Chungking), Rs. 3/-, 1944.
A semi-official publication, giving a picture of China under the intolerable stress of a prolonged war, fought single handed, against overwhelming odds.

WAR AND POLITICS IN CHINA by Sir John Pratt (Cape), 8/6, pp. 287, 1943.
A British diplomat long resident in China writes candidly about his experiences, often with humour.

---

## FOR DETAILED STUDY

---

CHINA by Rene Grousset (Civilisation of the East, Vol. 3), (Hamish Hamilton), 25/-, pp. 363, 1934.

CHINA by L. A. Lyall, (Ernest Benn) Modern World Series, 21/-, pp. 353, 1943.

INVASION OF CHINA BY THE WESTERN WORLD by E. R. Hughes, (A. & C. Black), 15/-, pp. 323, 1937.

THE INNER HISTORY OF THE CHINESE REVOLUTION by Tang Leang Li (Routledge), 15/-, pp. 391, 1930.

KUOMINTANG AND THE FUTURE OF THE CHINESE REVOLUTION by T. C. Woo, (Allen & Unwin), 15/-, pp. 278, 1928.

CHINA, SPAIN AND THE WAR by Jawaharlal Nehru, (Kitabistan), Rs. 2/8, pp. 269, 1940.

PROBLEMS OF THE CHINESE REVOLUTION by Leon Trotsky, (Pioneer Publishers, N.Y.), $4.00, pp. 432, 1932.

THE TRAGEDY OF THE CHINESE REVOLUTION by H. R. Isaacs (Secker & Warburg), 18/-, pp. 502, 1938.

REVOLUTION & COUNTER-REVOLUTION IN CHINA by M. N. Roy, (Renaissance Pub.) Re. 1/-. 1941.

RED STAR OVER CHINA by Edgar Snow, (Gollancz), 10/6, 1937.

SCORCHED EARTH by Edgar Snow, (Gollancz), 10/6, 1937.

SOVIET ATTITUDE TOWARDS CHINA by Stanley Powell (N. M. Tripathi: Bombay), pp. 99, 1945.

MY YEARS IN CHINA by Hallet Abend, (Lane), 12/6, 1944.

DAWN WATCH IN CHINA by Joy Homer, (Collins), 12/6, 1941.

PRESS AND PUBLIC OPINION IN CHINA by Lin Yu-Tang, (Oxford), 8/6, pp. 184, 1937.

CHUNGKING DIARY by D. F. Karaka, (Thackers, Bombay), Rs. 6/14, pp. 223 1942, 5th Impression, 1944.

MANCHURIA: CRADLE OF CONFLICT by Owen Lattimore, (Macmillan), $3.00.

MONGOLIAN JOURNEY by Owen Lattimore, (Cape) 12/6, 1941.

GATEWAY TO ASIA: SINKIANG by Martin R. Norins (John Day), $2.75, 1944.

TIBET by David MacDonald, (Oxford Pamphlet on Indian Affairs), Six Annas, 1945.

LHASA: THE HOLY CITY by F. Spencer Chapman (Readers Union), 3/6, 1940. Illus.

## *BIOGRAPHICAL NOTE*

The two outstanding leaders of modern China are Sun Yat-Sen and Chiang Kai-Shek. Dr. Sun's autobiography, *Memoirs of A Chinese Revolutionary,* is full of interest. The two best books on his life are Lyon Sherman's rather critical *Sun Yat-Sen* and *Strange Vigour: Life of Sun Yat-Sen* by Bernard Martin. Dr. Sun's three Principles of the People are discussed in his *San Min-Chu I.*

Hollington Tong's *Chiang Kai-Shek* easily remains the best biographical account of the Chinese Generalissimo. *Chiang Kai-Shek: Asia's Man of Destiny* by H. H. Chang is another interesting study. A shorter one is *Generalissimo Chiang Kai-Shek* by Phillip Paneth. *The Soong Sisters* by Emily Hahn gives the lives of Mesdames Sun Yat-Sen, Chiang Kai-Shek and Kung. An extremely interesting biographical-cum-descriptive study is *Autobiography of A Chinese Girl* by Hsieh Ping-Ying. *Battle Hymn of China* by Agnes Smedley gives the experiences of a well-known Communist writer.

## *OF LITERARY INTEREST*

Pearl Buck's *The Good Earth* secured for her the Nobel Prize. The triology *The Good Earth, The Sons* and *The House Divided* is now available in one volume under the title *The House of Earth. Storm Over Shanghai* by Andre Malraux is a novel of revolutionary China in 1927. Two lively collections of short stories are *Traditional Chinese Tales* and *Contemporary Chinese Stories*: 1908-1937 both translated by Chi Chen Wang, and each containing 20 stories. To these must be added another volume *Living China* edited by Edgar Snow. *A Moment in Peking* by Lin Yu-Tang is a work of major importance, while the same writer's *A Leaf in the Storm* is a vivid picture of the Chinese people facing the challenge of Japanese invasion. Other interesting titles include *Monkey* by Wu Chen-En, a sort of Chinese Pilgrim's Progress, and *Oil For the Lamps of China* by A. T. Hobart. *The Patriot* and *Dragon Seed* are two other really fine novels of Pearl Buck on the present situation. For a glimpse of Chinese literature see *Etchings of A Tormented Age* by Hsiao Chien (P.E.N.). *Lady Precious Stream, Bridge of Heaven* and *Spinners of Silk,* all by that gifted writer, S. I. Hsiung give an inimitable picture of both traditional and modern China.

---

# JAPAN

## INTRODUCTORY

JAPAN by Inazo Nitobe, (Ernest Benn), Modern World Series, 18/-, pp. 398, 1931.

The most comprehensive single book on Japan. Deals with the geographical features, historical background, the political and economic conditions, the constitutional structure, educational machinery and cultural progress.

JAPAN'S EMERGENCE AS A MODERN STATE by E. H. Norman, (Institute of Pacific Relations, New York), pp. 254, 1940.

A valuable study of the development of the Japanese State from the Meiji restoration in 1868 to the period of the Russo-Japanese War in the early years of the present century. Also deals with the peculiarities that influenced modern Japanese economic and political life and foreign policy.

JAPAN: ITS WEAKNESS AND STRENGTH by Kamaladevi, (Padma), Ans. 12/-, pp. 72, 1943 Reprinted 1944.

A balanced appraisal of conditions in Japan by a well known political and literary figure. Written after a personal visit. Chapters: Sun Over the Land of Rising Sun; Blossoms, Light and Music; Social Currents; Japan Builds Industries, The "New Order", The Pacific Blitz.

## FOR FURTHER READING

THE SOCIAL AND ECONOMIC HISTORY OF JAPAN by Ejiro Honjo, (Institute for Research in Economic History of Japan, Kyoto), 1935.

A standard work, by an eminent Japanese Professor, rich in quotation from original sources.

JAPAN OVER ASIA by W. H. Chamberlin (Duckworth), 8/6, pp. 328, Revised 1942, Illustrated.

An important and comprehensive book by a well-known American correspondent.

REPORT FROM TOKIO by Joseph C. Grew, (Hammond), 2/6, 1943.

TEN YEARS IN JAPAN by Joseph C. Grew (Hammond),, 15/-, 1944.

An interesting report by a career diplomat who was United States Ambassador to Tokio from 1932 to the attack on Pearl Harbour. This has been further elaborated in a later and fuller book *Ten Years in Japan* full of facts and lessons of the appeasement decade.

HELL IN THE SUNSHINE by Cedric Dover, (Secker & Warburg), 12/6, 1943.

A survey of Japan's rise to power in the Orient and her clash with Russia, China, Great Britain and the United States. The danger of Japanese propaganda on the oppressed colonial peoples, the world over is strikingly described in the second half of the book.

WAR AND DIPLOMACY IN THE JAPANESE EMPIRE by Takeuchi Tatsuji, (Allen & Unwin), 16/-, pp. 505, 1936.

An unassuming but all-important book. Describes the foundations and workings of the different departments of the Japanese State, the conduct of foreign relations, the clash between civilian control and military domination. The author, a Professor at Kwansi University, gives facts, but does not offer definite conclusions.

TRAVELLER FROM TOKIO by John Morris, (Cresset Pr.), 12/6, pp. 163, 1943. (Readers' Union) 3/6. The story of a British writer who was not arrested when Japan declared war in 1941. Description of life in Japan—the people, their food, education, marriage, literature, and the arts. Next, events from the outbreak of war to July 1942, when he was permitted to leave Japan.

---

## FOR DETAILED STUDY

---

JAPAN: A SHORT CULTURAL HISTORY by G. B. Sansom, (Cresset Pr.), 30/-, 1931, Revised 1943.

JAPAN by Rene Grousset, (Civilisation of the East Series, Vol. 4), (Hamish Hamilton), 25/-, pp. 341, 1936.

OUTLINE HISTORY OF JAPAN by H. H. Gowan & J. Washington Hall, (Appleton Century), 15/-, pp. 458, 1939.

GOVERNMENT IN JAPAN by C. B. Fahs, (Inst. of Pacific Relations, N.Y.) (Allen & Unwin), 5/-.

JAPAN SINCE 1931 by Hugh Borton, (Inst. of Pacific Relations), (Allen & Unwin), 6/6.

EYES ON JAPAN by General V. Yakhontoff, (Coward-Macmann), $3.50, 1936.

JAPAN'S FEET OF CLAY by Freda Utley, (Faber), 15/-, pp. 393, 1936.

MADE IN JAPAN by Guenther Stein, (Metheun), 7/6, pp. 206, 1935.

JAPAN'S DREAM OF WORLD EMPIRE, (Tanaka Memorial), Edited by Carl Crow, (Allen & Unwin), 5/-, 1943.

WITH JAPAN'S LEADERS by Fred Moore (Chapman & Hall), 15/-, 1943.

LITERATURE OF JAPAN by J. Ingram Bryan, (Home University Library), 3/-, pp. 256, 1929.

## *BIOGRAPHICAL NOTE*

*Life of Hideyoshi* by Walter Denning; *The Maker of Modern Japan: Tokugawa Iyeyasu* by A. L. Sadler; Yamagata and Ito, the two rival statesmen who between them modernised Japan, in *Eminent Asians* by Upton Close; *Prince Sayonji,* the last of the elder Statesmen, by Y. Takekoshi; Finally, *The House of Mitsui,* published by the firm, a record of three centuries of Japan's leading financial firm. Among other things, they financed the military restoration of the Emperor in 1868, acted as court bankers from 1707, and issued currency notes, and helped to make and unmake ministries.

---

# THE FAR EAST

## INTRODUCTORY

AN A.B.C. OF THE PACIFIC by Dorothy Woodman, Penguins), 9d., pp. 192, 1942.
Outlines the background in which the battle of Asia was fought. Accounts of China and her history of Japan and her amazing transformation, of Burma, Indo-China, Thailand, the British, Dutch and American empires in the Far East and how British and American policy fostered Japanese militarism during the half century. A frank, sincere and outspoken book.

THE STORY OF THE PACIFIC by Van Loon, (Harrap), 8/6, pp. 315, 1940. Illustrated.

THE FIGHT FOR THE PACIFIC by Mark J. Gayn, (Lane), 10/6, pp. 378, 1941.

RAMPARTS OF THE PACIFIC by Hallet Abend, (Lane), 12/6, 1942.

FUTURE OF SOUTH-EAST ASIA by K. M. Pannikar, (Allen & Unwin), 5/-, pp. 96, 1943.

AN EXPLANATORY ATLAS OF THE FAR EAST by G. F. Hudson & Martha Rachman, (Faber), 8/6, pp. 143, 1942.

## COUNTRY BY COUNTRY

BURMA by Ma Mya Sein, (Oxford Pamphlets on Indian Affairs), Annas 6/-, pp. 32.

NEW BURMA by W. J. Grant, (Allen & Unwin), 7/6, pp. 157, 1940.

BURMESE DAYS by George Orwell, (Penguin) 9d.

CEYLON by H.A.J. Hulugalle, (Oxford Pamphlets on Indian Affairs) Annas 6/-, pp. 32.

CEYLON UNDER BRITISH RULE: 1795-1932 by Professor Lennox A. Mills, (Oxford), pp. 311, 1933, Map.

CEYLON by Lord Holden, (Allen & Unwin) pp. 315, 1939.

DUTCH EAST INDIES: ITS GOVERNMENT, PROBLEMS AND POLITICS by Amry Vandenbosch (Wm. B. Berdmans Pub. Co. Michingan, U.S.A.) $3.00, pp. 385, Map, 1933, Revised 1943.

FRENCH INDO-CHINA by Virginia Thompson, (Allen & Unwin) pp. 517, 1937, Map.

KOREA LOOKS AHEAD by A. J. Grazdanzev, (Institute of Pacific Relations), 25 cents, pp. 62, 1944.

MODERN KOREA by A. J. Grajdanzev, (John Day), $4.00, 1944.

MALAYSIA by Prof. Rupert Emerson, (Macmillan), 1937

BRITAIN AND MALAYA by Sir R. Winstedt, (Longmans), 1/-, pp. 80, 1944. (Illus.)

POST-MORTEM ON MALAYA by Virginia Thompson, (Macmillan), $3.00, pp. 323, 1943.

MANCHURIA (see China).

MONGOLIA (see China).

THE PHILIPPINE PROBLEM by W. H. Anderson, (Putnam) 1939.

THE PHILIPPINES: A Study in National Development by J. R. Hayden, (Macmillan), $5.00, 1942.

SIAM IN TRANSITION by K. P. Landon, (Oxford), 10/6, pp. 340, 1939.

MYSTERIES OF THAILAND: GREEN PRISON by Leigh Williams, (Thacker) Rs. 9/12, pp. 256, 1944.

TIBET (See China).

## *FOREIGN CORRESPONDENTS*

In *Retreat in the East* by O. D. Gallagher, (Harrap) 8/6, 1942, the loss of Malaya, Singapore and Burma are described frankly by the War Correspondent of the *Daily Express,* London. *Retreat With Stilwill* by Jack Belden (Cassell) 12/6, 1943, is good reporting and brilliant interpretation. The white man's defeat in Burma the author attributes "to the inherent contradiction of Britain as an imperialist, colonial power attempting to wage war on Fascism". *Red Moon Rising* by George Rodger (Cresset Press), 12/6, 1943, gives the experiences of one of America's leading photographers, who was also correspondent for *Life* in Burma. Apart from outspoken comment, there are 64 excellent full page illustrations.

# THE ARAB WORLD

## INTRODUCTORY

HISTORY OF THE ARABS by Philip K. Hitti, (Macmillan), 31/6, pp. 767, 1937, 3rd Ed. 1943.

A comprehensive and scholarly history from ancient times to the 16th century. The first hundred pages are devoted to the pre-Islámic period, then follows the rise of Islam, the conquest of Syria, Iraq, Persia, etc., the rise and fulfilment of the Omayyad and Abbasid empires, the conquest of Spain, and the glories of Baghdad, Damascus, Cairo, Cordova, and Granada. Interesting discussion on literary and scientific progress.

THE ARABS by Bertram Thomas (Butterworth), 5/-, pp. 372, 1937, Reprint 1940, Illustrated.

A sympathetic and competent history of Arab achievement in polity and the Arts and Sciences. A valuable background book.

ARAB CIVILISATION by Joseph Hell, (Mohomed Ashraf, Lahore), Rs. 6/-, pp. 140, 2nd Ed. 1943.

A sympathetic history by a German scholar. Contents: Arabia Before Islam, Mohamed, Muslim Conquest, The Omayyads, Baghdad, Muslim North Africa and Spain.

ARAB AWAKENING by George Antoninus, (A. & U) 18/-, 1938.

The story of the Arab national movement by a well-known Christian Arab writer whose recent death is a great loss. An important book.

MEET THE ARAB by John Van Ess, (John Day), $3, 1943.

'Shrewd analysis, lightened by personal reminiscenes, of the Arabs, by a life-long student and devoted friend of that people' (Foreign Policy Bulletin).

THE SEVEN PILLARS OF WISDOM by T. E. Lawrence, (Garden City Publishing Co.), $1.98.

'It is a superb story. The narratives of raids and counter-raids, inconceivably long marches across the desert, attacks, intrigues and retreats, make a tale as thrilling as any that has been written since Homer. Seven Pillars gives us nearly all of Lawrence as person and Lawrence as historic force . . . and make no mistake about it, it is an important book.' (Vincent Sheean).

ISLAM TO-DAY Edited by A. J. Arberry & Rom Landau (Faber), 12/6, pp. 258, 1943.

An informative symposium, but of uneven interest. The first part deals with the Arab countries, including the Empire of Ibn Saud, Iraq, Syria, Palestine, Trans-Jordan, Modern Egypt, Sudan, Lybia, Morocco etc., The second part is concerned with Persia, Afghanistan, India and Malaysia.

## ARABIA

ARABIA by St. John Philby, (Ernest Benn), Modern World Series, 15/-.

The course of Arabian history and civilisation treated with knowledge and sympathy by a noted authority.

SOUTHERN GATES OF ARABIA by Freya Stark, (Penguin), 9d.

Extremely readable and interesting.

IBN SAUD: LORD OF ARABIA by H. C. Armstrong, 1934, (Penguin), 9d.

A picturesque biographical study of the Puritan King of Arabia.

A LITERARY HISTORY OF ARABIA by Prof. R. A. Nicholson.

## IRAQ

IRAQ by Seton Lloyd (Oxford Pamphlet on Indian Affairs) Annas 6/-, pp. 32, 1944.
Brief, readable, pro-British.

IRAQ by Gertrude Bell, (Ernest Benn) Modern World Series, 15/-.
Written by one of the most distinguished authorities on the Near and Middle East, the book is both authoritative and informative, and gives a good insight into the historical and cultural trends in Iraq.

THE MAKING OF MODERN IRAQ by H. A. Foster, (Williams & Norgate), 15/-, pp. 319, 1936.
A history of Iraq from 1915 to 1935, by an American writer. Some chapters: Arab and Iraqi; Western Control and Eastern Revolt; Colony, Mandate or Treaty Great Britain Becomes Trustee in Iraq; The Struggle For Mosul Oil; Terminating the Mandate. There is also a short historical background.

## PALESTINE AND TRANS-JORDAN

PALESTINE—THE REALITY by J. M. N. Jeffreys, (Longmans), 12/6, 1939.
The realities of the situation in Palestine as affecting both the Arabs and the Jews presented with great force.

THE ARAB MOVEMENT IN PALESTINE AND ITS ORIGINS by Michael Assaf, (Davar, Tel-Aviv), pp. 86, 1936.
The rise of the Arab Nationalist Movement discussed in five lectures. Very useful.

THE FORGOTTEN ALLY by Pierre Van Paasen (Dial Pr.), $2.75, pp. 343, 1943.
The case of the Jews against the Arabs, presented with great skill by the author of *Days of Our Years*.

GREAT BRITAIN AND PALESTINE (Royal Inst. of Int. Affairs), 2/6, pp. 111, 1937.
A resume of British relations with Palestine during the last two decades. The full text of the Palestine Mandate is included.

A HANDBOOK OF PALESTINE AND TRANS-JORDAN by Sir Henry C. Luke & E. Keith-Roach (Macmillan), 16/-, 3rd Edition, 1943.

A handy and useful book of reference.

## SYRIA

THE NATIONALIST CRUSADE IN SYRIA by Elizabeth MacCallum, (Foreign Policy Assn. Report, N.Y.) 1928. 25 cents.

A brief analysis of the factors making for unrest in Syria.

LETTERS FROM SYRIA by Freya Stark, Edited by Sir Sydney Cockerel, (Murray), 9/-.

A glimpse of life in Syria by a well-known traveller-writer, roaming about the country in a most unconventional fashion.

ECONOMIC ORGANISATION OF SYRIA by S. B. Himadeh (American Univ., Beirut, Lebanon), 10/-.

A discussion of the economic life and structure of Syria by a writer who has also made similar studies of Iraq and Palestine.

NOTE.—Also consult *Syria As It Is* by Helen C. Gordon, *Turkey and Syria Reborn* by H. Armstrong and *Lebanon in Turmoil* by J. F. Scheltma.

## EGYPT

(See under AFRICA)

# IRAN

PERSIA by Sir Arnold Wilson, (Ernest Benn), 18/-, pp. 380, 1932.
A comprehensive work which deals with various aspects of life in Iran, the Country and the People; Agriculture; Commerce and Industry; Communications; Foreign Relations; Literature; Judicial System; Currency and Finance; Educational Traditions; etc.

MODERN IRAN by L. P. Elwell Sutton, (Routledge), 12/6, 1941.
An account of modern Iran giving information about history, economic conditions, and social and cultural progress.

REZA SHAH by Essad Bey, (Hutchinson), 18/-, 1936.
An interesting biographical appraisal of the late ruler of Iran. The writer is full of admiration for the reforms and modernisation of the country achieved by Reza Shah.

IRAN: Test of Relations between Great and Small Nations by Prof. Christina P. Grant. (Foreign Policy Association Report), 25 cents. April 15, 1945.
Interesting light on Iran's Oil resources and the crisis in her relations with Soviet Russia and Britain.

## FOR FURTHER READING

THE STRANGLING OF PERSIA: 1910-1911 by W. Morgan Schuster, (Appleton Century), 12/6, 1912.

A frank and courageous expose of the British and Tsarist Russian efforts to divide Iran into spheres of influence. The writer, an American, held a high post in the Persian Ministry and writes from first hand knowledge.

UNVEILED IRAN by Angela Rodkin, (Hutchinson), 9/6, pp. 158, 1942, 32 Illustrations.

A non-political travel book. An interesting account of a journey by car from Bushire to Shiraz, Isfahan, Teheran and the industrial belt.

---

## FOR DETAILED STUDY

---

A HISTORY OF PERSIA by Sir Percy Sykes (Macmillan), 2 Vols., £2-2, pp. 563 and 615, 3rd Ed. 1930.

REPORT ON ECONOMIC CONDITIONS IN IRAN, by S. Simons (H. M. Stationery Office, London) 1935.

FAMOUS CITIES OF IRAN by Lawrence Lockhart 1939.

THE VALLEY OF THE ASSASSINS by Freya Stark, (Murray), 3/6, pp. 319, 1934.

LITERARY HISTORY OF PERSIA by Prof. E. G. Browne 3 Vols.

PRESS AND POETRY OF MODERN PERSIA by Prof. E. G. Browne.

## AFGHANISTAN

A HISTORY OF AFGHANISTAN by Sir Percy Sykes, (Macmillan), 2 Vols., £2-10, 1940. Maps and Illustrations.

The standard history of Afghanistan.

AFGHANISTAN: A BRIEF SURVEY by Jamaluddin Ahmed & Mohommad Abdul Aziz, (Luzac, London), 15/-, pp. 180, 1934.

Primarily a reference book, well illustrated. It reveals Afghanistan as being well along the road to modernisation.

AFGHANISTAN: FROM DARIUS TO AMANULLAH by Sir George MacMunn, (Bell), 21/-, pp. 359, 1929.

An able survey from a pro-British point of view.

# EUROPE

## ENGLAND

### INTRODUCTORY

BRITAIN AND THE BRITISH PEOPLE by Ernest Barker, (Oxford), World To-day Series, 3/6, pp. 141, 1942.

A brief sketch by an eminent writer, who is Professor of Political Science in Cambridge. It deals with the characteristics of the British people, the genius of her parliamentary institutions, the system of government, of law, the church, education and the social services.

THE ENGLISH PEOPLE by D. W. Brogan, (Hamish Hamilton), 10/6, pp. 260, 1943.

A book seeking to explain the Englishness of England. A discussion and description of many sides of English life. Comparison between English and American political and social institutions is a striking feature. "By far the soundest study of the English people produced during the last three decades". (Manchester Guardian).

ENGLAND SINCE THE INDUSTRIAL REVOLUTION by J. Hampden Jackson, (Gollancz), 4/6, pp. 312, 1936.

Summarises the industrial history of England from 1815. A readable and stimulating introductory volume.

THE BRITISH COMMON PEOPLE: (1746-1938) by G. D. H. Cole & Raymond Postgate, (Metheun), 6/-, pp. 691, 1938. 24 maps and charts.

Two hundred years of British history, with the common people on the centre of the stage. Written in simple English, by two of England's leading social thinkers.

---

## FOR FURTHER READING

---

ENGLAND by Dean Inge, (Ernest Benn), Modern World Series, 15/-, pp. 302, 1926.

An arresting picture of England against the background of the modern world, written from a conservative point of view. On its first appearance it was described as 'a creditable failure in an important task'. Bright and scholarly.

PARLIAMENTARY GOVERNMENT IN ENGLAND by H. J. Laski, (Allen & Unwin), 12/6, pp. 453, 1938.

A brilliant and erudite study of the pre-requisites on which Parliamentary Government in England and its working depends. An extremely able introductory chapter is followed by those on The Party System, The House of Lords, The House of Commons, The Cabinet, The Civil Service, the Judiciary, and the Monarchy.

ENGLISH SOCIAL HISTORY: A SURVEY OF SIX CENTURIES by G. M. Trevelyn, (Longmans), 21/-, 1944.

A comprehensive survey of English social history from Chaucer to Queen Victoria—a picture of life in its manifold aspects—social structure, religion and the arts, commerce and trade. Without social history, says the writer, "economic history is barren and political history is unintelligible." An important book by a great scholar and writer, who is Master of Trinity College, Cambridge.

THE THIRTIES IN GREAT BRITAIN (1930-40) by Malcolm Muggeridge, (Hamish Hamilton), 9/6, pp. 327, 1940.
A sparkling and provocative commentary on a decade of events in Great Britain and beyond, spiced with anecdotes about high and mighty in politics, social life and literature.

THE ENGLISH: ARE THEY HUMAN? by G. J. Renier, (Williams & Norgate) 7/6, pp. 286, 1931.
A witty and satirical portrayal of the English, their character, their traditions, and their institutions, by a Dutch writer.

INSIDE THE LEFT—THIRTY YEARS OF PLATFORM, PRESS, PRISON AND PARLIAMENT by A. Fenner Brockway, (Allen & Unwin), 15/-, pp. 352, 1942.
Ostensibly the autobiography of a well-known Socialist leader, in reality a political and social chronicle of great intrinsic value. It throws much interesting light on the Socialist movements in Great Britain and outside and on their leading personalities. A number of political letters of Bernard Shaw appear for the first time in the volume.

THE BRITISH EMPIRE—ITS STRUCTURE AND SPIRIT by Eric A. Walker, (Oxford), Royal Inst. of Int. Affairs, 12/6, pp. 250, 1943, Reprinted 1944. (Map).
History of the British Empire from its beginning 350 years ago. Four-fifths of the book is devoted to the events of the past century. The matter on India is very self-righteous, and sometimes misleading.

---

## FOR DETAILED STUDY

---

A HISTORY OF THE ENGLISH PEOPLE by J. R. Greene, (Everyman's Library) 2 Vols., 3/-, each 1874. (Supplement upto 1914).

A HISTORY OF THE ENGLISH PEOPLE SINCE 1815 by Elie Halevy, (Pelicans), 6 Vols., 9d. each.

A PEOPLE'S HISTORY OF ENGLAND by A. L. Morton, (Gollancz), 7/6, 1938.

HISTORY OF BRITISH CIVILISATION by Esme Wingfield-Stratford, (Routledge), 25/-, pp. 1352, Revised 1940.

POLITICAL THOUGHT IN ENGLAND 4 Vols., (Home University Library), 3/-, each.

A CONSTITUTIONAL HISTORY OF MODERN BRITAIN: (1985-1937) by Lindsay Kerr, (A. & C. Black) 20/-, 2nd Ed., 1943.

THE LAW OF THE CONSTITUTION by A. V. Dicey, (Macmillan), 12/6, pp. 577, Several Editions.

PARLIAMENT by Ivor Jennings, (Cambridge University Pr.), 25/-, 1939.

CABINET GOVERNMENT by Ivor Jennings, (Cambridge University Pr.), 21/-, pp. 484, 1936.

GREAT BRITAIN FROM ADAM SMITH TO THE PRESENT DAY: An Economic and Social Survey by C. R. Fay, 1940.

ENGLAND: (1870-1914) by R. C. K. Ensor, (Oxford), 15/-, pp. 660, 1936.

THE WORLD CRISIS by Winston Churchill (5 Vols.), Abridged 1 Vol. Ed., (Butterworth), 18/-, pp. 831, 1941.

A HISTORY OF BRITISH SOCIALISM by Max Beer, (Allen & Unwin) 15/-.

PRACTICAL SOCIALISM FOR BRITAIN by Hugh Dalton, (Routledge) 3/6, pp. 401, 1935.

BRITAIN IN THE POST-WAR WORLD by G. D. H. Cole, (Gollancz), 6/-, 1942.

THE DECLINE AND FALL OF THE BRITISH EMPIRE by Robert Briffault, (Simon & Schuster, N. Y.), $2, pp. 264, 1938.

SURVEY OF BRITISH COMMONWEALTH AFFAIRS by W. K. Hancock (Royal Inst. of Int. Affairs), Vol. 1, 25/-, Vol. 2 (Part I, 15/-, Part II, 16/-), 1942.

A SHORT HISTORY OF THE BRITISH COMMONWEALTH by Ramsay Muir, (Phillips), Vol. 1, 16/-, pp. 815; Vol. 2, 17/6, pp. 898.

SERVING MY TIME: AN APPRENTICESHIP IN POLITICS by Harry Pollitt, (Lawrence & Wishart), 5/-, pp. 292, 1940.

GUILTY MEN by "Cato", (Gollancz), 3/6, pp. 125, 1940, 42nd Impression 1944.

THE BRITAIN I WANT by Emanuel Shinwell, (Macdonald), 10/6, pp. 216, 1943.

BRITISH LIFE AND BRITISH THOUGHT (Symposium), British Council, (Longmans, Green), 8/6, 1944.

THE BEVERIDGE REPORT ON SOCIAL SECURITY (H. M. Stationary Office), 2/-, pp. 299, 1942. An attractive exposition of the Report will be found in *Beveridge Explained* by G. D. H. Cole, (Vora: Bombay), Re. 1, 1944.

---

## *BIOGRAPHICAL NOTE*

Among the recent studies of contemporary leaders, the following may be recommended: *Mr. Churchill* by Phillip Guedella, *My Early Life* by Winston Churchill, *Churchill* by Robert Sencourt; *Stafford Cripps—Advocate and Rebel* by Patricia Strauss; *Anthony Eden* by A. C. Johnson. Among the older biographies are *Great Victorians* Edited by H. J. & Hugh Massingham; (Penguin), *Queen Victoria* by Lytton Strachey; *Gladstone* by Lord Morley; *Disraeli* by Andre Maurois; (Penguin) *Robert Owen* by G. D. H. Cole; *Asquith* by Spender & Asquith *Lloyd George* by Sir E. Mallet; *Ramsay MacDonald* by Lord Elton; *My Apprenticeship* by Beatrice Webb (Penguin); *Bernard Shaw* by Hesketh Pearson; *Experiments in Autobiography* by H. G. Wells, *Testament of Youth* by Vera Brittain and *Confessions and Impressions* by Ethel Mannin (Penguin).

---

# FRANCE

## INTRODUCTORY

FRANCE by Jacques Metadier, (Macdonald), 5/-, 1944.
A brief introductory volume by a well-known French writer.

FRANCE IS A DEMOCRACY by Louis Levy, (Gollancz), 5/-, pp. 158, 1944, Intro. by H. J. Laski.
Glimpses of French history from 1815 to the present day. A description of the country and the people. An account of the French Parliament, especially of the parties and groups of the Left. The author is a prominent member of the French Socialist Party.

DEVELOPMENT OF MODERN FRANCE, (1870-1939) by D. W. Brogan, (Hamish Hamilton), 21/-, pp. 744, 1940.
A scholarly and comprehensive account of Modern French History, from the fall of the Second Empire to the outbreak of World War II.

FRANCE: THE BIRTH OF THE FOURTH REPUBLIC by Maurice Edelman, (Penguin), 9d. pp. 122, 1944.
An appraisement of the French Committee of National Liberation and of its leader General De Gaulle. A topical book.

## FOR FURTHER READING

FRANCE by Sisley Huddleston, (Benn) Modern World Series, 15/-, pp. 613, 1927.

Supplies the necessary background, but the approach is moderate and cautious. Written with sensitiveness and with real affection for the French people and their civilisation.

POLITICAL THOUGHT IN FRANCE FROM SIEYES TO SOREL by J. P. Mayer, (Faber), 8/6, pp. 148, 1943.
A history of French political thought from the Revolution of 1789 to the fall of the Third Republic. Extensive bibliography.

THE HEART OF FRANCE by George Slocombe, (Hutchinson), 5/-, pp. 225, Undated.
Offers an insight into the mind of the French peasantry, describes the beauty of the countryside, and the political, literary and Bohemian Paris of the days since the first World War. Also a stimulating chapter on the Genius of France.

THE LAST DAYS OF PARIS by Alexander Werth (Hamish Hamilton), 10/6, 1940.

THE BATTLE OF FRANCE by Andre Maurois, (Lane), 7/6, pp. 210, 1941.

A THOUSAND SHALL FALL by Hans Habe, (Harrap), 10/6, pp. 281, 1943.

PARIS UNDERGROUND by Etta Shiber, (Harrap), 10/6, 1944.

THE ARMY OF SHADOWS by Joseph Kessel, (Cresset Press), 7/6, pp. 166, 1944.

THIS IS NOT THE END OF FRANCE by Gustav Winter, (Allen & Unwin), 12/6, pp. 299, 1943.
A group of interesting books giving vivid details about the fall of France and its aftermath. The military debacle, the callousness of the ruling clique, the corruption of politics, the demoralisation and the disorganisation that followed, seem too amazing to be true. Through misfortune many remained true to the Spirit of France. Also an assessment of the forces at work for the restoration of a strong post-war Republican France.

## FOR DETAILED STUDY

HISTORY OF FRENCH PEOPLE by J. Seignobos, (Cape), 12/6, pp. 412, 1933.

THE FRENCH REVOLUTION by J. M. Thompson (Basil Blackwood), 32/6, 1943.

THE FRENCH REVOLUTION by A. Mathiez, (1928).

LECTURES ON THE FRENCH REVOLUTION by Lord Acton.

THE SOCIALIST TRADITION IN THE FRENCH REVOLUTION by H. J. Laski, (Fabian Society) 1/-.

THE PARIS COMMUNE OF 1871 by Frank Jellinek, (Gollancz), 7/6, pp. 447, 1937.

POST-WAR FRANCE by Paul Vaucher, Home Univ. Library, 3/-, pp. 256, 1934.

THE ECONOMIC POLICY OF FRANCE by G. Peel, (Macmillan), 1937.

I WILL NOT REST by Romain Rolland, (Selwyn & Blount), 8/6, pp. 320, 1936.

THREE YEARS OF FIGHTING FRANCE, (1940-43) by Felix De Grand' Combe, (Wells, Gardener and Darton), 3/6, 1944.

THE FRENCH COLONIES, PAST AND FUTURE by Jacques Stern, (Didier, N.Y.), $3, pp. 352, 1944, (10 maps).

LANDMARKS IN FRENCH LITERATURE by Lytton Strachey, (Home Univ. Library), 3/-.

A SHORT HISTORY OF FRENCH LITERATURE: FROM THE MIDDLE AGES TO THE PRESENT DAY by Lawrence Bisson, (Penguin), 9d. pp. 159, 1943.

## *BIOGRAPHICAL NOTE*

*Napoleon* by Emil Ludwig and *Napoleon* by H. A. L. Fisher are probably the two best biographies; *Jean Jaures: His Life and Work* by J. Hampdon Jackson is the life of "the greatest of all democratic Socialists". Other titles *Clemenceau* by Jean Martet; *Leon Blum: From Poet to Premier,* by R. L. Stokes; *De Gaulle: A Giant In The Age of Steel* by Count A. A. Hessenstein. *The Two Marshals: Bezain and Petain* by Phillip Guedella. Three other books of exceptional interest are: *Romain Rolland* by Stefan Zweig, *Madame Curie* by Eve Curie, *Call No Man Happy,* the autobiography of Andre Maurois. Three other very interesting little books in Cassell's Living Thoughts Library are *Montaigne* by Andre Gide, *Rousseau* by Romain Rolland and *Voltaire* by Andre Maurois. Another stimulating study of *Voltaire,* is by H. N. Brailsford in the Home Univ. Library. Rousseau's '*Confessions*' called 'the frankest autobiography in the world' is available in the Everyman's Edition. The latest study of *Romain Rolland* is by A. Aronson.

# GERMANY

## INTRODUCTORY

THE GERMANS by Emil Ludwig, (Hamish Hamilton), 12/6, pp. 399, 1942.

'The book is intended to be a history not of Germany, but of the Germans, with reverence for the German spirit but with censure for the German State. This discrepancy between the State and Spirit distinguishes German history from that of all nations'. (p. 5).

THE NAZI DICTATORSHIP by F. L. Schumann, (Knopf), $3.50, pp. 516, 1935 (Revised 1939).

"This is the definite work on Hitlerism, practically perfect of its kind." (E. A. Mowrer).

OUR SETTLEMENT WITH GERMANY by H. N. Brailsford, (Penguins), 9d., pp. 176, 1944.

A courageous book advocating 'a tolerable future for the German people'.

## FOR FURTHER READING

GERMANY by G. P. Gooch, (Benn), Modern World Series, 15/-, pp. 360, 1935.

One of the best books for the background of pre-1914 Germany, together with a valuable description upto 1925. Contains an interesting analysis of the Treaty of Versailles.

THE BIRTH OF THE GERMAN REPUBLIC by Alfred Rosenburg, (Oxford), 15/-, pp. 298, 1931.

A HISTORY OF THE GERMAN REPUBLIC by Alfred Rosenburg, (Methuen), 15/-, 1936.

*The Birth of the German Republic* deals with the internal events in Germany before and during the war that led to the revolution of 1918. The other traces the vicissitudes of the following years, the framing of the Weimer constitution, the inflation, the Dawes and the Young plans, the collapse of the economic system in 1930, and the events leading to the victory of Hitler.

MEIN KAMPF by Adolf Hitler, (Reynall & Hitchkock, N.Y.), $3.75, pp. 1050, 1939. Also a badly abridged Edition (Hurst & Blackett), 3/6, pp. 285.

Hitler's autobiography.

GERMANY'S REVOLUTION OF DESTRUCTION by Hermann Rauschning, (Henemann), 10/6, pp. 317, 1939.

A widely publicised book by the ex-Nazi President of the Danzig Senate. 'It is hard to give any adequate idea of the magnitude and the riches of this book—not extravagant to compare it with Burke's *Reflections on the French Revolution*' (Ernest Barker).

AUTOBIOGRAPHY OF A GERMAN REBEL by Toni Sender, (Labour Book Service), 2/6, pp. 305, 1940.

'*The Autobiography of a German Rebel* is more than an autobiography. It is, I am inclined to think, the best study of post-war Germany from the Socialist point of view that I have read'. (Herbert Morrison in the Preface.)

THE FAILURE OF A MISSION by Sir N. Henderson, (Hodder & Stroughton), 7/6, 1940.

AMBASSADOR DODD'S DIARY (Gollancz), 12/6, 1941.

BERLIN DIARY by William Shirer, (Hamish Hamilton), 12/6, 1941.

LAST TRAIN FROM BERLIN by Howard K. Smith, (Cresset Press), 10/6, 1942.

BEHIND THE STEEL WALL by Avid Fredborg, (Harrap), 10/6, 1944.

A series of reports that have preserved for us a vivid picture of Germany since the advent of Hitler. The first two respectively by the British and American Ambassadors to Germany, and the other three by three well known foreign correspondents.

---

## FOR DETAILED STUDY

---

HISTORY OF GERMANY by Hermann Pinnow, (Dent), Everyman's Library, 3/-, 1929. Translated by H. N. Brailsford.

FROM BISMARCK TO THE WORLD WAR by E. Brandenburg, (Oxford), 15/-.

GERMANY'S THREE REICHES by E. Vermeil, (Andrew Dakers), 18/-, 1945.

DER FUHRER—HITLER'S RISE TO POWER by Konrad Heiden, (Gollancz), 10/6, 1944.

THE GERMAN ECONOMY, (1870-1940) by G. Stolper, (Allen & Unwin), 1940.

HOW NAZI GERMANY HAS CONTROLLED BUSINESS by L. Hamburger (Brookings Institution, Washington), (Faber) 5/-.

I PAID HITLER by Fritz Thyssen, (Hodder), 8/6, pp. 314, 1941.

THE NEW GERMANY by a Group of Refugee German Socialists, (Penguin), 9d. 1943.

BISMARCK by Emil Ludwig, (Putnam), 7/6.

WILLIAM II by Emil Ludwig, (Putnam), 7/6.

I WAS A GERMAN by Ernest Toller, (Lane) 5/-, pp. 294, 1936.

LETTERS FROM PRISON by Ernest Toller, (Lane), 15/-, (1936).

## *OF LITERARY INTEREST*

When in the prevailing hysteria of war, the cry for total revenge on Germany is loud in the air, it is important not to forget that it was Germany which gave to the world, Goethe and Schiller, Kant and Schopenhauer, Beethoven and Wagner, Marx and Engels, Mann and Einstein.

Goethe's towering contribution to the world of letters may be studied in his own works, in Eckermann's *Conversations With Goethe* (Everyman's Library), and in the biographical studies of George Brandes and Emil Ludwig. There are delightful chapters on Kant and Schopenhauer in Will Durant's *Story of Philosophy,* and brief monograms on *Kant* by Julian Benda and on *Nietschze* by Heinrich Mann in The Living Thoughts Library. And what more delightful book can one hope for than *Beethoven* by Romain Rolland? Klaus Mann's *The Turning Point—Twenty-Five Years in this Century,* gives a vivid picture of the life of the Manns in the days of their glory in Germany.

# ITALY

## INTRODUCTORY

ITALY YESTERDAY, TO-DAY & TOMORROW by Paolo Treves, (Gollancz), 4/6, pp. 128, 1942.

A brief and attractive survey of events in Italy from 1870 to the present day. The writer has been a well-known leader of the Italian Socialist Party.

ITALY by Luigi Villari, (Ernest Benn), Modern World Series, 18/-, pp. 392, 1929.

A scholarly description of Italian history from the French Revolution to 1929. Half the book is devoted to recent history, which is presented through Fascist spectacles.

THE FRUITS OF FASCISM by Herbert L. Mathews, (Harcourt Brace) $3, 1943.

"This is easily the best account of the rise and decline of Italian Fascism available in the English language. The only work of comparable depth and seriousness is Hermann Finer's *Mussolini's Italy.* And *Fruits of Fascism* is better written and more up-to-date, bringing the story to the eve of Mussolini's downfall. Uncommonly good book." (Atlantic Monthly).

## FOR FURTHER READING

THE DEVELOPMENT OF MODERN ITALY by C. J. S. Sprigge, (Duckworth), 10/6, pp. 216, 1943.

One of the most readable books on modern Italy—from the unification of the country under the House of Savoy to the rise of Mussolini in the early twenties. The diplomacy of Cavour, the idealism of Mazzini, the daring of Garibaldi, and the part of each in the making of modern Italy and their conflicts and disagreements are put in their proper setting.

MUSSOLINI'S ITALY by Hermann Finer, (Gollancz), 18/-, pp. 564, 1935.
Brilliantly exposes the myth of the 'Corporative State'.

MY AUTOBIOGRAPHY by Benito Mussolini, (Hutchinson Pocket Library), 6d., pp. 252, (Undated).
A vivid and colourful account of the life of the former Italian Dictator.

---

## FOR DETAILED STUDY

---

THE LEGACY OF ROME, Edited by C. Bailey, (Oxford), 8/6, pp. 524, 1923.

HISTORY OF ITALY: From Pre-Historic Times to the Present Day by L. Salvatorelli, (Allen & Unwin), 25/-, pp. 688, 1940.

HISTORY OF ITALY: (1871-1915) by Benedetto Croce (Oxford) $3, 1942.

ABYSSINIA AND ITALY (Royal Inst. of Int. Affairs), 2/-, pp. 55, Third Ed. 1935, Map.

BALCONY EMPIRE: FASCIST ITALY AT WAR by Reynalds & Eleanore Packard (Oxford)·12/6, 1942.

ITALY FROM WITHIN by Richard G. Massock, Chief of Associated Press, Rome Bureau. (Macmillan), 15/- pp. 352, 1943.

THE VATICAN: YESTERDAY, TO-DAY & TOMORROW by George Seldes, (Kegan Paul), 15/-.

FOREIGN POLICY OF THE VATICAN by Sherman Hayden, (Foreign Policy Association), 15th January, 1944, 25 cents.

ETERNAL CITY: ROME OF THE POPES by D. Holisher, (Ungar Pub. Co., N.Y.), $3, pp. 160, 1943, 228 Illustrations.

MUSSOLINI'S ROMAN EMPIRE by G. T. Garratt, (Penguin) 9d.

---

## *BIOGRAPHICAL NOTE*

*Mazzini* by Boulton King and *Garibaldi* by G. M. Trevelyan are both well known. *Mazzini* by Carlo Sforza (Living Thoughts Library) is full of interest. Of the various books on Mussolini, George Seldes' *Sawdust Caesar* is full of eloquent condemnation, while Sir Charles Petrie's *Mussolini* is a sympathetic account. *One Man Alone* by Maxwell H. H. Macartney holds Mussolini responsible for the Italian catastrophe.

## *LITERARY FOOTNOTE*

*The Mother* by Grazzia Delleda won the Nobel Prize (1926). Luigi Pirandello achieved the same distinction a few years later (1934). His *Six Characters in Search of An Author* and *The Naked Truth* are justly famous. Ignazio Silone's *Fontamara, Bread and Wine* and *Seed Beneath the Snow* are three widely discussed anti-Fascist novels. Benedetto Croce's historical and philosophical works are famous, especially his *History As the Story of Liberty* and *History of Europe in the XIXth Century*. A volume on Pareto by Dr. Franz Borkenau will be found in Modern Sociologists Series, (Chapman & Hall), Pareto's *Mind & Society* is also available in an English translation.

---

# SCANDINAVIA

THE SMALLER DEMOCRACIES by Sir E. Simon (Gollancz), 6/-.

A compact and stimulating book, full of shrewd and sympathetic comment. Depicts a highly developed civilisation, without poverty or unemployment, and extensive social services.

## DENMARK

DENMARK: THE CO-OPERATIVE WAY by F. C. Howe, (Coward McCann, N.Y.), $2.50, pp. 293, 1936.

'Co-operation is the very texture of life, not a thing apart; it is the Danes' equivalent for Socialism.' The present volume brings down to date the writer's earlier book *Denmark: A Co-operative Commonwealth, Ruled by Farmers.*

## FINLAND

FINLAND: THE NEW NATION by Agnes Rothary (Faber), 12/6, pp. 257, 1936.

An enthusiastic traveller's account, that is much more than a travel book.

FINLAND by J. Hampden Jackson. A very competent book by a noted authority.

## NORWAY

NORWAY: A HANDBOOK (Dent), pp. 196, 1944 (price not stated).

A handy, informative little book issued under the auspices of the Information Office of the Norwegian Government.

NORWAY by G. Gathorne Hardy (Modern World Series) Benn, 12/6. A full account of the Land of the Midnight Sun by a well-known authority.

## SWEDEN

DEMOCRATIC SWEDEN Edited by Margaret Cole & Charles Smith, (Routledge), 6/-, 1938.
A symposium to which a number of well-known writers contribute. An attractive picture of a working democracy.

SWEDEN—THE MIDDLE WAY by Marquis W. Childs (Yale Univ. Pr.) $2.50, 1936.
A remarkable book. The author shows how the Middleman who is generally responsible for high prices, has been succesfully eliminated in Sweden.

STALWART SWEDEN by Joachim Joestin, (Doubleday Doran), $2.75, 1943.
A readable account of the recent developments in Sweden by a Scandinavian journalist, now the Assistant Editor of the *Newsweek*.

SCHOOL FOR LIFE: A Study of the Peoples Colleges of Sweden by F. Margaret Foster, (Faber), 6/-, 1944.
An enthusiastic review of an extremely significant movement—the *Folkhogskolor*—residential colleges for the adults, of which there are 60 in Sweden. There are no examinations and no prescribed syllabus, all receiving State aid but developing on their own line.

## *OF LITERARY INTEREST*

There has been quite a flowering of literature in the Scandinavian countries. The Plays of Ibsen had profound influence in Europe and far beyond, to a lesser extent the Plays and Poems of Bjornson. Selma Lagerloff (Sweden), won the Nobel Prize in 1909. Her chief novels are *Gosta Berling's Saga* and *The Outcast.* Verner Von Heidenstam (Sweden) was awarded the Nobel Prize in 1916. *The Carlists* and *St. Brigitta's Pilgrimage* are his best known works. *Kristin Lavransdatter* by Sigrid Undset (Norway, Nobel Prize, 1928) is a triology consisting of *The Garland, The Mistress of Husaby* and *The Cross. Fridolin's Garden* by E. A. Karlfeldt (Sweden), Nobel Prize 1931, *The Pilgrim Kamanita* by Karl Gjellerup (Denmark), Noble Prize jointly with Henrik Pontoppidan: (Denmark) *The Promised Land, Fallen Asleep While Young* by F. Silenpaa (Finland), Nobel Prize, are other titles. Knut Hamsun (Norway), Nobel Prize 1920, whose *Growth of the Soil, Hunger* and *The Vagabond* are famous, is now facing trial for collaboration with Hitler. *The Shining Sea* by Kjerstin Goransen-Ljungman, was awarded the prize for the best Swedish novel published in 1943.

*Scandinavian Plays of The Twentieth Century,* (First and Second Series), edited by A. Gustafson, (Princeton Univ. Pr.) $5/-, 1945 are interesting without being outstanding.

Bernard Shaw accepted the Nobel Prize but not the prize money. This he gave away for the specific purpose of facilitating translations of important literary works from the Scandinavian languages into English, with a view to promote a better understanding between the countries.

# SOVIET RUSSIA

## INTRODUCTORY

RUSSIA by Sir Bernard Pares, (Penguins) 9d., pp. 256, 1941.

A pleasantly written compendium on Russia from the 9th century to the present day.

SOVIET RUSSIA: AN INTRODUCTION by K. Gibberd, (Royal Inst. of Int. Affairs), 1/-, pp. 80, 1942.

A useful introductory volume which gives in bare outline the political and social institutions of the U.S.S.R., with a number of maps and diagrams.

RUSSIA: A SOCIAL AND CULTURAL HISTORY by D. S. Mirsky, (Cresset Pr.) 16/-, pp. 338, 1931.

An invaluable study of the Russian temperament. A study of Russian history and of her political and economic institutions. The book comes up to 1917, but the period between 1862 and 1917 receives rather inadequate treatment, only 40 pages being devoted to it. Good illustrations.

HISTORY OF THE RUSSIAN REVOLUTION by Leon Trotsky, (Gollancz), 10/6, pp. 1295, (1932).

The history of the Revolution by one of its leading participants. Covers the period from February to November 1917. It is as much the history of the Revolution, as a treatise on revolutionary sociology, and deals with the philosophy of history, the problem of nationalities, the relationship between the peasantry and the urban proletariat.

SOVIET RUSSIA: ANATOMY OF A SOCIAL HISTORY by E. Strauss, (Lane), 12/6, pp. 342.

"This impressive book describes the transformation of Russia and the Communists during the full period 1917 to 1941. It offers a reasonably complete history with a minimum of statistical data and explains the complicated relation between the development of Soviet society and the various changes in Communist policy."

THIRTY MONTHS IN RUSSIA by D. G. Tendulkar, (Karnatak Pub. House), Rs. 1-8, pp. 96, 1943. Illustrated.

Attractive and readable. An intellectual's personal record of 30 months in the Soviet Union.

---

## FOR FURTHER READING

---

MY REMINISCENCES OF THE RUSSIAN REVOLUTION by M. Phillip Price, (Allen & Unwin), 7/6, pp. 402, 1921.

THROUGH THE RUSSIAN REVOLUTION by Albert Rhys Williams, (Labour Pub. Co., London), 5/-, pp. 311, 1923.

TEN DAYS THAT SHOOK THE WORLD by John Reed, (Modern Library), 95 Cents. Also Modern Book Shop, 2/6, pp. 322, 1926. With a Preface by Lenin.

Three eye-witness accounts of the Russian Revolution of 1917. Each book is distinctive and supplements the information in the other two. They are all enthusiastic accounts.

HUMANITY UPROOTED by Maurice Hindus, (Cape), 6/-, pp. 370, 1929.

Brilliantly depicts the impact of the new social order on men and institutions of changing Russia.

SOVIET COMMUNISM: A NEW CIVILISATION? by Sidney & Beatrice Webb, (Longmans), 2 Vols., 35/-, pp. 1257, 1935. 3rd Ed., 1941. (1 Vol. Ed., 30/-, 1944).

Acclaimed as the best book on Soviet Russia in the English language. Also criticised by non-Communists, as written from books and not from personal knowledge of Russian conditions or Russian language and based largely on official Soviet sources, which the authors accepted without sifting. The Webbs at the age of 80, spent four years in writing this book.

RUSSIA'S IRON AGE by W. H. Chamberlain, (Duckworth), 15/-, pp. 389, 1935.

Covers the period from 1928 to 1934 and is a detailed survey of the events of those days, especially of the Second Five-Year Plan.

MEN AND POLITICS by Louis Fischer, (Cape), 18/-, pp. 639, 1941.

A remarkable personal testament by a noted authority on international affairs. Only a part of the book deals with Russia, where the writer spent 14 years. Pungent remarks on the Stalin-Trotsky controversy, the Trials, and the foreign policy of the Soviet Union and its interactions on the Spanish Civil War. Two sections of the book have been separately published in India, *Lenin's Russia* and *Stalin's Russia* (Padma Publications, 12 annas each.)

MISSION TO MOSCOW by Joseph E. Davies (Gollancz) 16/-, pp. 318, 1942.

A very favourable picture of the Russian scene by the American Ambassador to Moscow from 1936 to 1938. The book largely consists of official despatches sent from time to time to the State Department and selections from his diary and correspondence. It has also been filmed.

MOSCOW DATELINE by Henry C. Cassidy, (Cassell), 10/6, 1943.

RUSSIA AT WAR by Ilya Ehrenburg, (Hamish Hamilton) 10/6, 1943.

THE RUSSIAN CAMPAIGNS OF 1941-1943 by W. E. D. Allen & P. Muratoff (Penguins), 9d., 1944.

MOTHER RUSSIA by Maurice Hindus, (Collins), Rs. 10/8, pp. 355, 1943. (Readers Union, 3/6).

LENINGRAD by Alexander Werth, (Hamish Hamilton) 10/6, 1944.

A budget of highly interesting and topical books on the Soviet-German war, describing the progress of the war through its various phases, its ups and downs, the scorched earth policy, the sacrifice of the guerilla warfare and the magnificent resistance of the Red Army.

---

## ADDITIONAL REFERENCES

---

A HISTORY OF RUSSIA by Sir Bernard Pares, (Cape), 21/-, pp. 570, 3rd Ed., 1938.

INTRODUCTION TO RUSSIAN HISTORY by B. H. Summer, (Duckworth), 16/-, 1943.

PICTORIAL HISTORY OF RUSSIA—FROM RURIK TO STALIN by A. Howard & E. Newmann, (Hutchinson), 14/6, pp. 207, 1944, Five hundred illustrations.

A BRIEF HISTORY OF RUSSIA by M. N. Pokrovsky, (Martin Lawrence), 2 Vols., 6/-, each, pp. 295 and 348, 1933.

NAPOLEON'S INVASION OF RUSSIA, 1812 by Eugene Tarle (Allen & Unwin), 12/6, pp. 300, 1943.

THE U.S.S.R.: AN ECONOMIC AND SOCIAL SURVEY by S. P. Turin, (Methuen), 16/-, 1944.

A SHORT HISTORY OF THE U.S.S.R. by Walter Duranty, (Hamish Hamilton), 12/6, 1944.

RUSSIAN ECONOMIC DEVELOPMENT SINCE THE REVOLUTION by Maurice Dobb (Routledge), 15/-, pp. 437, 1929.

SOVIET ECONOMY AND THE WAR by Maurice Dobb, (Routledge), 3/6, pp. 88, 1941.

SOVIET MONEY AND FINANCE by L. E. Hubbard (Macmillan), 12/6, 1936.

THE RUSSIAN PEASANT by Sir John Maynard, (Gollancz), 15/-, pp. 512, 1942.

IN SEARCH OF SOVIET GOLD by John D. Littlepage & Demaree Bess (Harrap), 8/6, pp. 287, 1939.

I WENT TO THE ARCTIC by Ruth Gruber, (Gollancz), 10/6, pp. 380, 1939.

BEHIND THE URALS by John Scott, (Secker & Warburg), 7/6, pp. 223, 1942.

SOVIET ASIA: ITS RECORD AND ITS PROBLEMS by E. S. Bates, (Cape), 8/6, pp. 192, 1942.

SOVIET ASIA by R. A. Davies & A. J. Steiger (Gollancz), 7/6, pp. 205, 1943, Map.

SEVEN SOVIET ARTS by Kurt Landon, (Faber), 15/-, pp. 381, 1937. Illustrated.

SOVIET RUSSIAN LITERATURE by G. Struve, (Routledge), 4/6, pp. 270, 1935.

THE NEW SOVIET THEATRE by J. Macleod, (Allen & Unwin), 12/6, pp. 242, 1943.

---

### *NOTE*

A mass of literature has grown up attacking Stalinism. The leading critic was Leon Trotsky; among his books are *The Real Situation in Russia* (Allen & Unwin), 7/6, pp. 364, 1928, *The Revolution Betrayed* (Faber), 10/6 pp. 312, 1937, *The Third International After Lenin* (Pioneer, N. Y.) $3, pp. 357, 1937, and *Stalin's School of Falsification* (Pioneer, N.Y.), $2.50, pp. 326, 1937. Another well-known critic is Max Eastman, whose viewpoint will be found in *Stalin's Russia And the Crisis in Socialism,* (Allen & Unwin), 7/6, pp. 272, 1940 and *Artists in Uniform,* (Allen & Unwin), 7/6, pp. 261, 1934. Andre Gide's *Back From the U.S.S.R.* (1937) and *Afterthoughts On the U.S.S.R.* (1938) both (Secker), 2/6 each, are a record of impressions after a personal visit to Russia. Among other books are *Assignment in Utopia* by Eugene Lyons,

*From Lenin to Stalin* by Victor Serge, *I was Stalin's Agent* by General Krivitsky, *Out of the Night* by Jan Valtin, and *The Dream We Lost* by Freda Utley, *Report On The Russians* by W. L. White. An unsual novel *Darkness At Noon* by Arthur Koestler deals with the Treason Trials.

## BIOGRAPHICAL NOTE

The definitive life of Lenin still remains to be written. *Lenin* by D. S. Mirsky, *Lenin* by Valeru Marcu, *Lenin*, (Marx-Engels-Lenin Inst., Moscow), together with *Memoirs of Lenin* 1893-1917 by his wife N. Krupskaya and *Days With Lenin* by Maxim Gorky, enable us to get a correct picture of the great revolutionary.

A glowing life of Stalin is *Stalin* by Henri Barbusse. *Landmarks in the Life of Stalin* by E. Yaroslavski and *Stalin: A Short Biography* (Marx-Engels-Lenin Inst., Moscow), and *Stalin* by J. T. Murphy are eulogistic accounts. *Stalin: A Critical Survey* of Bolshevism by Boris Souvarine and *Stalin* by Isaac Don Levine are two highly critical studies. Stalin's *Leninism* and his *Marxism and the National and Colonial Question* are among his principal writings.

*Litvinoff* by Arthur Upham Pope, *Maisky: Ten Years Ambassador* by G. Bilainkin and *Before the Storm* the autobiography of Maisky, are of interest.

For Trotsky: his autobiography, *My Life* and *Trotsky: Portrait of a Youth* by Max Eastman. A brilliant but devastating sketch is in Winston Churchill's *Great Contemporaries. The Truth About Trotsky* by R. F. Andrews is a scathing attack from the official Communist view-point. *Assassination of Leon Trotsky* by Albert Goldman is by an ardent supporter.

For revolutionaries of an earlier generation see *Michael Bakunin* by E. H. Carr, *Memoirs* by Herzen, *Memoirs of A Revolutionary* by Kropotkin, and *Memoirs of a Revolutionist* by Vera Figner. Another book of outstanding interest is *Leo Tolstoy* by Aylmer Maude (World's Classics).

# SPAIN

## INTRODUCTORY

SPAIN by Salvador De Madariaga, (Ernest Benn), Modern World Series, 25/-, 1930, New Ed. 1943.

A scholarly history of Spain tracing her development upto the end of the Civil War, by a famous Spanish writer and statesman.

DIALOGUE WITH DEATH by Arthur Koestler, (Penguin), 9d.

Aspects of the Spanish Civil War. Partly autobiographical and partly imaginative writing, it is based on the author's earlier book *The Spanish Testament.*

APPEASEMENT'S CHILD: THE FRANCO REGIME IN SPAIN by Thomas J. Hamilton, (Gollancz), 7/6, pp. 239, 1943, 6th Imp. 1944.

The Franco regime under the searchlight, by the Madrid correspondent of the New York *Times.* On its publication, Franco's Ambassador in America protested to the State Department.

## FOR FURTHER READING

VIRGIN SPAIN: DRAMA OF A GREAT PEOPLE by Waldo Frank, (Duell, Sloane & Pearce), $3.50, 1926, New Ed. 1942.

THE SPANISH LABYRINTH by Gerald Brennan (Cambridge Univ. Pr.), 21/-, 1943.

SPAIN IN ECLIPSE: 1937-1943 by E. Allinson Peers, (Methuen), 15/-, 1943.

THE SPANISH COCKPIT by Franz Borkenau, (Faber), 7/6, pp. 303, 1937.

HISTORY OF THE SPANISH REPUBLIC by A. Ramos Oliviera, (Gollancz), 10/6, 1944.

---

## *BIOGRAPHICAL NOTE*

*Francisco Franco* by Joaquin Arraras is more eulogy than biography. The autobiography of Constancia de la Mora, *In Place of Splendour,* offers a panorama of the palace, the slum, the bitterness of the civil war and exile. *Freedom's Battle* by Alvarez del Vayo, Republican Foreign Minister at the time of the Civil War, is good picture of Spain during the stress of the upheaval. *Lorca: The Poet And His People* by Arturio Barea, is the life of the famous poet who was assassinated during the Civil War.

## *LITERARY FOOTNOTE*

Of the literary material about present-day Spain, the following are of special interest: *Seven Red Sundays* by Ramon Sanders, (Penguin), *Lean Men* by Ralph Bates (Penguin), 2 Vols. Two important novels of the Spanish Civil War are *Days of Hope* by Andre Malraux and *For Whom the Bell Tolls* by Ernest Hemingway. *The Spanish* Omnibus is a representative collection of short stories by leading Spanish writers. Arturo Barea's *The Forge* and *The Clash* have attracted much notice since their recent publication.

---

# TURKEY

## INTRODUCTORY

TURKEY by Barbara Ward, (Oxford), World To-day Series, 3/6, pp. 124, 1942. Illustrated.

A brief introductory volume dealing with both political and economic resources of the country.

MODERN TURKEY by John Parker & Charles Smith, (Routledge), 12/6, pp. 259, 1940.

A sympathetic account of present-day Turkey. Written after an extensive tour. Chapters on Anatolian Land and Peoples; The Fall of the Ottoman Empire; Kemal Ataturk; The Political Structure; Agriculture, Industrial Growth; Religious and Legal Change; Women Win Their Freedom; Education and the Arts; The Health Services; Foreign Policy; Military Power and Strategic Position; etc. An appendix gives the programme of the Republican People's Party. John Parker, one of the writers, is Director of the New Fabian Research Bureau, London.

GREY WOLF by H. C. Armstrong, (Penguin), 9d.

A highly dramatised but not very sympathetic life of Mustafa Kemal, which portrays him as a watchful but ruthless dictator.

TURKEY BETWEEN TWO WORLD WARS by Professor J. K. Birge, (Foreign Policy Association, N.Y.) 25 cents, (Report Nov. 1, 1944).

Compact, Informative and very readable.

## FOR FURTHER READING

TURKEY by A. Toynbee & K. P. Kirkwood, (Ernest Benn), Modern World Series, 15/-, pp. 329, 1926.

An authoritative history of New Turkey with a full background of the revolutionary events of 1919-1922. A very valuable book.

TURKEY by Emil Lengyel, (Random House), $4, pp. 474, 17 Illustrations & Maps, 1941.

"Not long ago Turkey's history was the history of all the peoples from the Atlantic Ocean to the Persian Gulf. We shall expose the highlights of her frequent wars and infrequent interludes of peace. We shall have a word to say about the Balkans, the Armenian Tragedy, the revolt in the desert, and the Arab question. At the end of our journey we shall face modern Turkey, the miracle of the East. The great statue of Mustapha Kemal Ataturk will have to be measured. Was he the motive power of New Turkey or merely her voice? Through him, perhaps we shall obtain a glimpse into the heart and mind of the New Turk." (p. 12).

A SPEECH by Mustapha Kemal, (K. E. Koelher, Leipzig), 42/-, pp. 724, 1929.

A document of unique interest. The entire volume consists of a speech delivered by Kemal before the Deputies and representatives of the Republican Party at Angora, giving the inner history of the Turkish Revolution and his share in it. The speech lasted for six days, from October 15 to 20, 1927. 'Gentlemen' I have taken trouble to show, in these accounts, how a great people, whose national course was considered ended, reconquered its independence; how it created a national and modern State founded on the latest results of science. This holy treasure I lay in the hands of the Youth of Turkey. Turkish Youth!

Your primary duty is ever to preserve and defend the National Independence, the Turkish Republic.' (p. 723).

ALLAH DETHRONED by Lilo Linke, (Constable), pp. 341, 1937. 81 Illus. (Travel Book Club Ed. 3/6). A book of adventurous travel by an unconventional European writer who went where she liked and saw what she pleased, and in any case had very little money to spend.

---

## FOR DETAILED STUDY

---

THE TURKEY OF ATATURK by D. E. Webster, (The American Academy of Political and Social Science) Philadelphia, $2.25, pp. 337, 1939.

THE MAKING OF MODERN TURKEY: FROM BYZANTIUM TO ANGORA by Sir Henry Luke (Macmillan) 10/6, 1936.

THE RISING CRESCENT: Turkey Yesterday, To-day, Tomorrow by Ernest Jackh, (Farrar & Reinhart), $3.50, 1944.

TURKEY: KEY TO THE PAST by C. M. Tobin, (Putnams), $2, pp. 170, 1944. Maps.

TURKEY AT THE STRAITS by J. T. Shotwell & Francis Deak, (Macmillan), $3.00, 1940.

THE DEVELOPMENT OF NATIONAL BANKING IN TURKEY, (Press Dept. of the Ministry of Interior, Ankara), 1938 (Price not stated).

## *BIOGRAPHICAL NOTE*

The best book on Kemal is *Mustapha Kemal: Between Europe and Asia* by Dagobert von Mikusch, a sympathetic, glowing account by a writer who knew him intimately. Professor H. R. Wortham's *Mustapha Kemel* is pleasant and very readable. *Kemal, the Maker of Modern Turkey* by Sirdar Iqbal Ali Shah is an enthusiastic journalistic appraisal. For figures of an earlier generation, see *Abdul Hamid* by Dr. Alma Wittlin (1940) and *Memoirs* of Djamal Pasha (1927), who along with Enver and Talaat Pashas led the Young Turk Revolt against Sultan Abdul Hamid. See also *Memoirs* of Halide Edib (1926) and her *Turkish Ordeal* (1928) which show us a new Turkey through the eyes of a noted woman leader.

# OTHER EUROPEAN COUNTRIES

## THE BALKANS

BALKAN BACKGROUND by Bernard Newman (Robert Hale), 15/-, pp. 288, 1944, Illus. & Maps.

A popularly written book, by the author of *New Europe* and other works, giving the historical background and a discussion of the complex social problems of the Balkan countries which have more than once jeopardised the peace of Europe.

THE BALKAN STATES (Royal Inst. of Int. Affairs), 7/6, pp. 194, 1938.

A review of the economic and financial developments of Albania, Bulgaria, Greece, Roumania and Yugoslavia since 1919.

THE LONG BALKAN NIGHT by Leigh White, (Scribner), $3.50, 1944.

A courageous document describing the Balkan countries during the present war. The author has been Balkan Correspondent of various important journals for eighteen years. Two other books of similar interest are *From the Land of the Silent People* by Robert St. John and *Balkan Journal* by Laird Archer.

BLACK LAMB AND GREY FALCON by Rebecca West, (Macmillan), 42/-, Revised 1943. (American Edn. $5.00 Viking Press).

'Probably the greatest book written since the war began' (Dorothy Thompson).

ECONOMIC DEVELOPMENT IN SOUTH-EASTERN EUROPE (P.E.P.) Oxford 10/6, pp. 166, 1944.

A group of experts on political and economic planning in the powder-magazine of Europe.

LIFE OF GREECE by Will Durant, (Simon & Schuster) $3.75, pp. 754, 1939.

A cultural book of permanent value and of exceptional interest.

## CZECHOSLOVAKIA

A SHORT HISTORY OF CZECHOSLOVAKIA by Kamil Krofta, (Williams & Norgate), 7/6.

A brief but excellent survey by a well-known authority.

A HISTORY OF CZECHS AND SLOVAKS by R. W. Seton Watson, (Hutchinson), 15/-, 1944.

Twelve hundred years of history, from the origins of the Bohemian State in the 7th Century to Hitler's march on Prague and the subsequent adventures of the Benes government in exile. A solid book by the greatest British authority on South East Europe.

---

### *BIOGRAPHICAL AND LITERARY FOOTNOTE*

Karel Capek's *Conversations With Masaryk* gives an intimate glimpse into the life of the first President of the Republic. Likewise *Benes* by Pierre Carbites is the life of the present head of the Czechoslovak government.

Capek remains *par excellence* the most eminent Czech writer. *Power and Glory, Insect Play, The Cheat;* these and some of his other writings belong to European literature. *The Unwilling Tourist* by Hoffman is a delightful book of refugee experiences, lavish in drawings. *To Sing With the Angels* is a powerful anti-Nazi novel by Maurice Hindus, while *Good Soldier Schweik,* (Penguin), is a masterpiece of satire.

---

## POLAND

A HISTORY OF POLAND by Oscar Halecky, (Dent), 15/-, 1942, Illustrated, Map.

A standard work by an outstanding Polish historian, gives eight hundred years of Polish history to 1941.

POLAND: BETWEEN TWO WARS by Dr. Ferdynand Zweig, (Secker & Warburg) 10/6, pp. 176, 1944.

Describes the vicissitudes of the Polish people in the two decades between World Wars I and II. Also an appraisal of her social and economic changes.

THE STORY OF A SECRET STATE by Jan Karski, (Hodder & Stroughton), 12/6, pp. 319, 1945. Remarkable story of the Polish Underground. A must book.

---

## *LITERARY FOOTNOTE*

Henryk Sienkiewicz was awarded the Nobel Prize in 1905. His best known works are *Quo Vadis* and *With Fire and Sword.* Another Nobel Prizeman is Wladyslas St. Reymont, (1924) whose chief works of fiction are *The Peasants* and *The Promised Land. Padareski* by Charles Phillips is the story of a modern immortal. See also *Polish Poetry,* Edited by Wanda Dynowska, and *Five Centuries of Polish Learning* by Prof. Stanislaw Kot. A number of informative booklets have recently been published by the Indo-Polish Library in Bombay.

---

## OTHER EUROPEAN COUNTRIES

MY AUSTRIA by K. Schussnigg, (Knopf), 1938.

SHOWDOWN IN VIENNA: THE DEATH OF AUSTRIA by Martin Fuchs, 1939.

THE BALTIC by J. Hampden Jackson (Oxford Pamphlets on World Affairs), 6d.

BELGIUM by R. C. K. Ensor, (Home Univ. Library), 3/-.

BELGIUM Ed. by J. Epstein, (Cambridge Univ. Press), 2/6, 1944.

THE MAKING OF MODERN HOLLAND by A. J. Barnouou, (Norton) $2.75, 1944.

HOLLAND by J. A. Veraart, (Macdonald), 5/-, 1944.

HUNGARY by Tibor Mende, (Macdonald), 5/-, 1944.

SALAZAR: BUILDER OF PORTUGAL by F.C.C. Egerton, (Hodder & Stoughton), 15/-, 1943. Very pro-Salazar.

HISTORY OF SWITZERLAND by W. Oechsli, (Cambridge Univ., Pr.) 20/- pp. 488, 1922.

# EIRE (IRELAND)

## INTRODUCTORY

A HISTORY OF IRELAND by Edmund Curtiss, (Methuen), 12/6, pp. 399, 1936.

Perhaps the finest history of Ireland available within the compass of a single volume. Scholarly, lucid, comprehensive and written in attractive style.

DE VALERA by Sean O'Faolain (Penguin), 9d.

A portrait of De Valera, the man and statesman and his contribution to the making of present-day Ireland.

## FOR FURTHER READING

THE EVOLUTION OF SINN FEIN, by R. M. Henry, (Talbot Press), Dublin, 5/-, 1925.

A masterly account of the rise of the Sinn Fein movement and of its thrilling vicissitudes, its innumerable difficulties, the determination of its leaders, and the sacrifices of the Irish people in the face of ruthless terrorism.

THE VICTORY OF SINN FEIN, by P. O'Hegarty, Talbot Press, Dublin, 5/-, pp. 219, 1924.

A moving account of the Irish revolt of 1916 and of the events that followed. "The insurrection of 1916 was a forlorn hope and a deliberate blood sacrifice. The men who planned it and led it did not expect to win. But they counted on being executed afterwards and they knew that THAT would save Ireland's soul. The European War had shown Ireland to be less Irish and more Anglicised than ever . . . and they offered up their lives as a sacrifice to recall the nation to heroic thought and heroic deeds to remind the people that they were a NATION and not a dependency. Never did any body of men go forth on a more desperate enterprise with purer hearts or a more unfaltering courage. When Tom Clarke faced the firing squad he knew that he had won. These May morning volleys blotted out the Old Ireland." (pp. 4-5).

## FOR DETAILED STUDY

THE IRISH REPUBLIC by Dorothy Macardle, (Gollancz), 25/-, Preface by President De Valera.

IRELAND'S BLOODLESS REVOLUTION: 1932-1936 by Rose S. Kelly, (Joyce & Smith, Chicago), $2, pp. 217, 1936.

IRELAND IN THE AGE OF REFORM & REVOLUTION by N. Mansergh, (Allen & Unwin), 1940.

THE STORY OF IRELAND by Sean O'Faolain, (Collins), Britain in Pictures Series, 4/-, pp. 48, 1943, with 8 colour plates and 22 other illustrations.

## *BIOGRAPHICAL NOTE*

Mr. De Valera stands out as the leading statesman of post-war Ireland. Of the several books written about him the latest is *Eamon De Valera* by J. MacManus. Two others that deserve special mention are *De Valera* by Dennis Gwynn and *Unique Dictator: A Study of Eamon De Valera* by Desmond Ryan. *Parnell* by St. John Irvine is now available in the Penguin Books, 9d.

*Michael Collins* by P. Beaslai 2 vols. is a vivid description of the life work of a great Irishman and the revolutionary struggles he led.

# U. S. A.

## INTRODUCTORY

THE AMERICAN PRIMER by Dorsha Hayes, (John Lane), 4/6, pp. 119, 1942.

U.S.A. by D.W. Brogan (Oxford), World Today Series, 3/6, pp. 144. Illustrated.

Two splendid introductory volumes.

THE EPIC OF AMERICA by James Truslow Adams, (Routledge), 8/6, pp. 446, 1932. Revised 1940. Illustrated.

America's national story, 'From time immemorial' to Roosevelt's New Deal, told with remarkable felicity and scholarship. Not only a colourful pageant of history, but also an attempt to discover 'how the ordinary American became what he is today in outlook, character and opinion.' (viii).

THE AMERICAN POLITICAL SYSTEM by D. W. Brogan, (Hamish Hamilton), 18/-, pp. 416, 1933, New Ed., 1943.

Prof. Laski calls this "the most illuminating treatise on American government since the late Lord Bryce's *American Commonwealth.*"

THE AMERICAN PRESIDENTS by Herbert Agar, (Eyre & Spotiswood), 6/-, pp. 135, 1936.

Lives of American Presidents from Washington to Harding. The book was awarded the Pulitzer Prize for biography.

U. S. FOREIGN POLICY by Walter Lippmann, (Hamish Hamilton), 6/-, pp. 109, 1943 (Thackers Rs. 3/8).

A brilliant and thought-provoking book by one of America's leading publicists.

## FOR FURTHER READING

**THE RISE OF AMERICAN CIVILISATION** by Charles & Mary Beard (Cape), 2 Vols. in 1, 30/-, pp. 824 and 865, 1927. Revised 1944.
Without doubt the most impressive single book on the United States. The first volume deals with the Agricultural Era, and the second with the Industrial Era. Indispensable for any student of international affairs. Three other books by the same writers and intended as a sequel, are: *America in Midpassage* 1919-1929 (Cape), 15/-, 1943, The *American Spirit,* (Macmillan) $5 pp. 674, 1942 and *The Republic* (Viking Pr.), $3, 1943, keep up a very high standard of writing.

**AMERICA: THE STORY OF A FREE PEOPLE** by Allen Nevins & Henry Steele Commager, (Oxford), 7/6, pp. 461, 1942.
A compact history of the American people by two of her well known historians.

**RECENT AMERICA** by Henry Bamford Parkes (Crowell), $3.50, pp. 664, 1941.
'The purpose of this book has been to describe the chief forces in the development of American society during the past forty years . . . the author has endeavoured to fill in the economic and social background . . . the growth of industrial corporations, the rise of Trade Unionism, the condition of agriculture . . . The intellectual and cultural changes have been examined in some detail . . . considerable attention has been given to foreign relations.' (Preface).

**ECONOMIC HISTORY OF THE UNITED STATES** by Chester W. Wright, (McGraw-Hill), 28/-, pp. 1120, 1941.

A comprehensive treatise on the development of economic life in the United States from the colonial period to 1940. There are 100 charts and maps and an adequate bibliography. Another good book is *American Economic History* by H. U. Faulkner, (Harper), $3.75, pp. 784, 1943.

THE AMERICAN PRESIDENCY by Harold J. Laski, (Allen & Unwin) 7/6, pp. 278, 1940.

A very able and lucid study. The author analyses the President's role *vis-a-vis* the Cabinet, the Congress, and the dual control of foreign relations. Laski pleads for more powers for the President.

THE HISTORY OF THE CONGRESS by Ernest Sutherland Bates, (Harper), 12/6, pp. 468, 1936.

A history of the American Congress from 1789 to 1935. A stimulating and refreshing book.

THIS IS CONGRESS by Roland Young (Knopf), $2.75, 1943.

A brief, realistic description of how the American Congress actually works.

DIPLOMATIC HISTORY OF THE U. S. by Samuel F. Bemis, (Holt), $5.50, 1942.

A comprehensive and scholarly history of American diplomacy.

STORY OF THE GREAT AMERICAN FORTUNES by Gustavus Myers, (Modern Library Giant), $1.45, pp. 732, 1936.

The title explains the scope of this famous book.

THE WAY OUT—WHAT LIES AHEAD FOR AMERICA by Upton Sinclair (Published by the Author, California) $1, pp. 108, 1933.

A series of nine letters, addresed to a young capitalist, warning him of what is coming and what he should do about it. Fulton Oursler, editor of *Liberty*, compares this book to Lincoln's Inaugural Address.

THE FLOWERING OF NEW ENGLAND by Van Wyck Brooks, (Modern Library Giant), $1.45, 1936.

A brilliantly written intellectual and literary history of the five decades during which Boston dominated American life and thought.

---

## FOR DETAILED STUDY

---

AMERICAN COMMONWEALTH by James Bryce, (Macmillan), 2 Vols., 42/-, pp. 742 and 962, 1888, Revised 1910.

POLITICAL AND SOCIAL GROWTH OF THE AMERICAN PEOPLE: 1865-1900 by A. M. Schlesinger, (Macmillan), 16/-, pp. 783, 1941.

STORM OVER THE LAND: A PROFILE OF THE CIVIL WAR by Carl Sandburg, (Cape), 12/6, pp. 250, 1943. (Readers Union), 3/6.

THE AMERICAN PROBLEM by D. W. Brogan, (Hamish Hamilton), 10/6, 1944.

THE HISTORY OF THE NEW DEAL by Basil Rauch, (Creative Age Pr.), $2.50, pp. 368, 1944.

THE ROBBER BARONS by Mathew Josephson, (Harcourt), $1.89, pp. 474, 1934.

FOLKLORE OF AMERICAN CAPITALISM by Thurman Arnold, (Yale Univ. Pr.) $3, pp. 400, 1937.

DECLINE OF AMERICAN CAPITALISM by Lewis Corey (Lane), 15/-, pp. 622, 1934.

AMERICAN SOCIALISM by H. W. Laidler, (Harper), $2.50, pp. 330, 1937.

CENTURY OF THE COMMON MAN by Henry A. Wallace, (Reynal), $1.50, pp. 96, 1943.

TENNESSEE VALLEY AUTHORITY: DEMOCRACY ON THE MARCH by David E. Lillianthal, (Penguins) 9d., pp. 208, 1944.

LEND-LEASE by E. R. Stettinius Jr. (Penguins), 9d., pp. 288, 1944.

THE STATE OF THE NATION by John Dos Passos, (Houghton-Mifflin), $2.75, 1944.

A TIME FOR DECISION by Sumner Welles, (Thackers, Bombay), Rs. 9-12, pp. 332, 1944.

SPEECHES AND DOCUMENTS ON AMERICAN HISTORY (Oxford), World Classics, 4 Vols. 3/- each

A HAND BOOK OF THE U.S.A. by the U.S. Office of War Information, (Hutchinson), 10/6, pp. 255, 1944.

MAIN CURRENTS IN AMERICAN THOUGHT by Vernon L. Parrington, (Three volumes in one). (Harcourt), $3.45.

THE GROWTH OF AMERICAN THOUGHT by Merle Curti, (Harper), $5, pp. 848, 1943.

THE STORY OF AMERICAN LITERATURE by Ludwig Lewisohn, (Modern Library Giant), $1.45 1937.

ON NATIVE GROUNDS AN INTERPRETATION OF MODERN AMERICAN LITERATURE by Alfred Kazin, (Cape), 21/-, pp. 541, 1943.

AMERICAN TESTAMENT by John Freeman, (Gollancz), 16/-.

---

## *THE NEGRO IN AMERICA*

While Paul Robeson and Marion Anderson, both world famous negro artists, by the beauty of their voice have captured the heart of America and make about a hundred thousand dollars a season, the negro problem remains one of the most crucial for American democracy. The latest book on the subject is *American Dilemma: The Negro Problem and American Democracy* by Gunnar Myrdal, Professor of Social Economy in the University of Stockholm, (Harper), 2 Vols., $7.50, 1944. This is an over-all study of the entire literature on the question published by the Carnegie Foundation. Another recent study ***What the Negro Wants*** edited by R. W. Logan, (Univ.

of N. Carolina), $3.50, pp. 352, 1944, gives the viewpoints of 14 leading Negro leaders, who demand equality in the American Community for the 13 million Negroes. *The Story of the Negro* by Booker T. Washington, (Peter Smith, N.Y.), 2 Vols., $5, pp. 332 and 437, 1940 and *The New Negro* by Alain Locke are two other authoritative studies. *The Negro's Share* by R. Sterner, (Harper), $4.50, pp. 433, 1943, is a study of income, consumption, housing and public assistance. Also see *Up From Slavery* Booker T. Washington's autobiography, (World Classics) and *George Washington Carver* by Rachham Holt, (Doubleday Doran), $3.50, 1943, the biography of the distinguished Negro scientist, one of the pioneers of scientific agriculture. *Black Boy* is the autobiography of the famous novelist, Richard Wright.

For their cultural activities see: *An Anthology of American Negro Literature* edited by V. F. Calverton, (Modern Library), 95 cents, *The Negro in Art,* edited by Alain Locke, and *The Negro Caravan* Edited by Sterling Brown, A. P. Davies and Ulysses Lee.

## *BIOGRAPHICAL NOTE*

*They Were Great Americans* gives the lives of 28 historic Americans by 28 contemporary Americans. Also see: *George Washington* by W. E. Woodward, *Thomas Jefferson* in the Living Thoughts Library, and *Jefferson Himself,* edited by Bernard Mayo, *Abraham Lincoln* by Carl Sandburg, and *Lincoln* by Emil Ludwig, *Woodrow Wilson and His Work* by W. E. Dodd, *Mr. Roosevelt* by Compton Mackenzie and *Roosevelt* by B. Doon.

Three studies of the financial barons are of particular interest, *My Life and Work* by Henry Ford, *The House of Morgan* by Lewis Corey, and *John D. Rockfeller* by Allan Nevins.

*Labour Baron: A Portrait of John L. Lewis* by A. Wechsler is a study of one of the most influential labour leaders, who seems to be perpetually in the maelstrom of controversy.

## *OF LITERARY INTEREST*

Pearl Buck, as President of the East & West Association, circularised noted personalities, asking them to name the 15 most important books by American writers, which would give a correct picture of the United States to a foreigner. • From a large number of replies the following were selected as the most representative:

FICTION: *Huckleberry Finn* by Mark Twain, *Tom Sawyer* by Mark Twain, *Little Women* by Louisa Alcott, *Main Street* by Sinclair Lewis, *Arrowsmith* by Sinclair Lewis, *My Antonia* by Willa Cather, *The Folks* by Ruth Suckow, *The Yearlings* by Marjorie K. Rawlings, *Grapes of Wrath* by John Steinbeck.

*Epic of America* by James Truslow Adams, *Rise of American Civilisation* by Charles & Mary Beard, *Our Times* by Mark Sullivan, *Flowering of New England* by Van Wyck Brooks, *Abraham Lincoln* by Carl Sandburg, *Leaves of Grass* by Walt Whitman. To us in India it seems most surprising that no book by Upton Sinclair is included. No American, and very few other writers, are as respected or as popular as Sinclair, in this country.

# SOUTH AMERICA

## INTRODUCTORY

INSIDE LATIN AMERICA by John Gunther, (Hamish Hamilton), 12/6, pp. 388, 1942.
On the same lines as the author's *Inside Europe* and *Inside Asia.* He takes us into all the countries of Central and South America.

GOOD NEIGHBOURS by Hubert Herring, (Yale Univ. Pr.) $3, 7th Printing 1943.
A scholarly and readable history of Argentine, Brazil, Chile and seventeen other South American countries.

PAN AMERICAN ECONOMICS by Professors P. R. Olson & C. A. Hickman, (Chapman & Hall), 27/-, pp. 479, 1943.
Explores the economic life of Latin America, with special emphasis on the composition and distribution of Pan American trade, the role of foreign capital, current foreign investments, tarriff policy, exchange control, Pan American co-operation and the future.

## COUNTRY BY COUNTRY

### ARGENTINE

A HISTORY OF ARGENTINE by Ricardo Levene, Univ. of North Carolina), (Oxford), 18/-, pp. 582.
A scholarly and sympathetic history of Argentine Republic.

ARGENTINE DIARY by Ray Josephs, (Random House), $3/-, pp. 404, 1944.

A lively book, written with vigour by an American foreign correspondent who has spent several years in Argentine. Another good book is: *The Argentine* Riddle by F. J. Weil.

## BRAZIL

BRAZIL: LAND OF THE FUTURE by Stefan Zweig (Cassell), 10/6, 1942.

An extremely well written account of Brazil. Brazil's land area is bigger than that of Europe and twice that of India, but the population is only forty-four millions. Stefan Zweig, world famous writer, draws attention to its untapped possibilities and calls it the land of the future.

## CHILE

CHILE by Augustin Edwards, (Benn), Modern World Series, 15/-.

Comparatively uneventful but not undisturbed past, the unsettled present, and an uncertain future—that is how a careful observer sees Chile.

## MEXICO

A HISTORY OF MEXICO by H. B. Parkes, (Allen & Unwin), 12/6, 1939.

Mexico's colourful history through the eyes of an American historian.

TIMELESS MEXICO by Hudson Strode (Harcourt Brace), $3.50, 1944.

"Probably the best book written on Mexico. It is a brilliant literary work, ethnologically fascinating and of great political merit." (Thomas Mann).

---

## *OF LITERARY INTEREST*

*Sunburst* by Mauricio Magdaleno, a novel, has been called Mexico's *Grapes of Wrath*. *Revolt on the Pampas* by Theodore Plivier is a splendid novel about Chile. Another work of fiction, about an Indian village community in the Peruvian Andes, is *Broad and Alien is the World* by Ciro Alegria. Four famous travel books are *Beyond the Mexique Bay* by Aldous Huxley, *Brazilian*

*Adventure* by Peter Fleming, *Tschifelli's Ride* by A. Tschifelli, and *South American Journey* by Waldo Frank.

Emil Ludwig's biography of Latin America's most famous leader *Simon Boliver*, Ricardo Roja's *San Martin*, the great South American liberator, and Salvador di Madariaga's *Hernan Cortez* conqueror of Mexico, are of interest. An extremely colourful and brilliant life of *Diego Rivera* Mexico's foremost artist, is by Bertram D. Wolfe. *Rebellion in the Backlands* (Os Sertoes) by Euclides da Cunha is a Brazilian masterpiece. 'It is one of those astonishing original works which appear from time to time, like a volcano on a flat plain, to remind us that man is not merely unpredictable but creative. There is nothing like it in Brazilian literature or in any other.' (*The Nation*). *The Green Continent* is a distinguished anthology by 33 of Latin America's leading writers, edited by G. Arciniegas.

---

## CANADA

CANADA by B. K. Sandwell, (Oxford), World To-day Series, 3/6, pp. 128, 1942.

An account of Canadian development from the status of a colony to that of a self-governing Dominion. Written by a well known Canadian.

CANADA TO-DAY AND TOMORROW by W. H. Chamberlin (Robert Hale), 12/6, 1944.

A survey of Canadian problems, with special emphasis on the result of the present war on Canadian economy, and their bearing on the future.

CANADIAN PROGRESSIVES ON THE MARCH by M. J. Coldwell, M.P., (League for Industrial Democracy, N.Y.) 15 cents, pp. 32, 1944.

The story of the rise of the Co-operative Commonwealth Federation of Canada told by its President, who is also the leader of the C.C.F. in the Canadian House of Commons.

CANADIAN ACCENT edited by Ralpf Gustafson, (Penguins), 9d., pp. 144, 1944.

An interesting selection of stories and poems by contemporary writers from Canada.

# AFRICA

## BACKGROUND BOOKS

THE RAPE OF AFRICA by Lamar Middleton, (Robert Hale), 12/6, at Rs. 7/-, pp. 288, 1936.

An inside political history of the scramble for territory on the part of seven European nations in Africa, over a period of sixty years. The author exposes the hypocrisy of the talk of "civilising the blacks" and traces the story of European aggression. Foreword by Leonard Barnes.

THE EMPIRE IN AFRICA by Alexander Campbell, (Gollancz), 6/-, pp. 160, 1944.

The author of *Smuts and Swastika* gives here a panoramic view of the various colonial areas of Africa, detailing their resources and possibilities. It is a clear account of what is wrong in Africa and what must be done about it.

BEHIND GOD'S BACK by Negley Farson, (Gollancz), 5/-, pp. 373, 1940, 15th Imp. 1944.

An eye-witness survey by a famous correspondent of an adventurous journey from coast to coast across Africa, covering South West Africa, South Africa, Tanganyika, Uganda, Belgian Congo, French Equatorial Africa, The Gold Coast, etc. His conclusions are pro-British. A very entertaining travel book.

AN AFRICAN SURVEY by Lord Hailey, (Royal Inst. of Int. Affairs), 21/-, pp. 1866, 1938.

A valuable study, pro-British in outlook, prepared by a Committee of the Royal Institute of International

Affairs, under Lord Hailey, giving a wide range of information on contemporary African questions.

---

## FOR FURTHER READING

---

HOW BRITAIN RULES AFRICA by George Padmore, (Wishart), 7/6, 1936.
An attack on the colonial system by a well known African leader. The author is very severe against the Boers. An important book.

THE BLACK MAN'S BURDEN by E. D. Morel, (National Labour Pr.) Manchester, 3/6, pp. 241, 1920.
A classic picture of 'the atrocious wrongs which the white people have inflicted on the black'. Chapters on: The Slave Trade, Invasion, Capitalistic Exploitation; Graphic description of events in Rhodesia, Morocco, Tripoli, and the Congo.

BRITISH IMPERIALISM IN EAST AFRICA AND BRITISH IMPERIALISM IN WEST AFRICA, (Labour Research Dept., London) 6d. each.

RACE AND POLITICS IN KENYA by Margery Pelham & Elspeth Huxley, (Faber), 12/6, 1944.

FACING MOUNT KENYA by Jomo Kenyetta, (Secker & Warburg), 12/6, pp. 339, 1938.

HISTORY OF SOUTH AFRICA: SOCIAL AND ECONOMIC by C. W. D. Kiweit, (Oxford), 15/-, pp. 304, 1941.

A HISTORY OF SATYAGRAHA IN SOUTH AFRICA by Mahatma Gandhi, (Navjivan Pr.) Rs. 4/-.

THE GOVERNMENT OF FRENCH NORTH AFRICA by H. J. Liebsny, (University of Pennsylvania Press U.S.A.) $1.50, 1943.

ETHIOPIA UNDER HAILE SELASSIE by Christine Sandford, (Dent), 10/6, 1944.

A HISTORY OF ABYSSINIA by A.H.M. Jones and E. Munro, (Oxford), 6/-, pp. 196, 1935.

## FOR DETAILED STUDY

PLAN FOR AFRICA by Rita Hinden (Allen & Unwin), 7/6, pp. 223, 1942.

CAPITAL INVESTMENT IN AFRICA by H. S. Frankel, (Oxford), 10/6, pp. 506, 1938.

EMPIRE AND COMMERCE IN AFRICA by Leonard Woolf (Hogarth Pr.), 7/6, 1920.

AFRICA ANSWERS BACK by Prince Akiki K. Nyabongo, (Routledge), 7/6, 1936.

WITHOUT BITTERNESS: Western Nations In Post-War Africa by A. A. Nivafor Orizu (Creative Age Press) $3, 1944.

AFRICA VIEW by Julian Huxley, (Chatto & Windus), 5/-, pp. 455, 1936.

GREY STEEL: LIFE OF FIELD-MARSHAL SMUTS by H. C. Armstrong, (Penguin) 9d.

### EGYPT

EGYPT by George Young, (Ernest Benn), Modern World Series, 15/-, pp. 352, 1927.

A picture of Egypt, historical, political and cultural, cleverly done with a pro-British bias. Also a restrained account of the boycott of the Milner Commission, the awakening among the students, and their part in the growth of the nationalist movement.

GREAT BRITAIN AND EGYPT, (Royal Inst. of Int. Affairs), 2/-, pp. 67, 1936.

The facts and relevant documents concerning the stormy relations between the two countries, from the beginning of World War I to 1936.

INDEPENDENT EGYPT by Amine Yussef Bey, (Murray), 10/6, pp. 272, 1940.

A political autobiography, written with diplomatic restraint. Describes events in Egypt since 1914. The author is the first Egyptian plenipotentiary to the United States of America.

THE SUEZ CANAL by Sir Arnold Wilson, (Penguin Books), 9d.

A romantic story of power politics.

---

## *LITERARY FOOTNOTE*

*Dark Testament* by Peter Abrahams, a collection of short stories and sketches by an African intellectual, 23 years old, born in a suburb in Johannesburg. Gives us in his stories the lives, hardships and philosophy of his people, the eight million dark South Africans. *African Discovery* Edited by Margery Perham & J. Simmons, is a very interesting collection of passages from the records of the more famous British explorers of Africa. The Editors supply introductions and brief biographical notes on the different explorers. Probably the best South African writer is Olive Schreiner. *The Story of An African Farm* (Penguin), is one of her best known stories. *The White Prophet* by Hall Caine, gives the story of the Mehdi Rebellion in Egypt, which was ultimately crushed by Lord Kitchener. An interesting account of General Gordon, who met his death in this rebellion, will be found in Lytton Strachey's *Eminent Victorians. Makers of South Africa* by B.L.W. Brett, (Foreword by Field Marshal Smuts) gives the development of South Africa as revealed in the lives of its famous men.

## *FOREIGN CORRESPONDENTS*

For World War II the following will be found of particular interest. *The Battle is the Pay Off* by Ralph Ingersoll. Editor of New York daily *P. M.*, (Lane), 7/6, 1943, and The *End In Africa* by Alan Moorhead, (Hamish Hamilton), 10/6, 1943. Also *The World Blackout* a diary of the first year of the present war, by the well known South African writer Sarah Gertrude Millin.

---

# AUSTRALASIA

## AUSTRALIA

THE AUSTRALIANS by A. L. Haskell, (A. & C. Black), 4/6, 1943.

An introductory volume by the author of *Waltzing Matilda,* giving a good account of Australia's rise to Nationhood.

AUSTRALIA by W. K. Hancock, (Ernest Benn), Modern World Series, 15/-, pp. 326, 1930.

A survey that is both competent and scholarly, giving due weight to political, economic and cultural factors. Chronology and maps.

AUSTRALIA, HER HERITAGE AND HER FUTURE by Paul Macguire, (F. A. Stokes, N.Y.), $3.50, pp. 349, 1939, 66 Illustrations.

A story of the growth and development of a continent, from a penal settlement to its present position.

## NEW ZEALAND

NEW ZEALAND: A WORKING DEMOCRACY by Walter Nash (Dent), 8/6, 1944.

'A picture of the smallest of the British Dominions by the New Zealand Minister to the United States.'

NEW ZEALAND: THE LAND OF MY CHOICE by Ellen Roberts, (Allen & Unwin), 10/6. Illustrations.

An enthusiastic description of New Zealand —her people, their way of life and institutions.

NEW ZEALAND'S LABOUR GOVERNMENT AT WORK by W. B. Sutch (League for Industrial Democracy, N.Y.) 15 cents., pp. 32, 1940.

Briefly but attractively summarises the work of the Labour Government in New Zealand.

# SOCIAL & POLITICAL TRENDS

## SOCIALISM

To the question: 'What books must one read on Socialism,' the typical 'capitalist' answer is, that there is no such thing as Socialism—there are numerous varieties of it and some of them are even at loggerheads with one another. How far is this true?

While the central idea of a society in which exploitation and poverty have been banished and in which the instruments of Production, Distribution and Exchange are socially owned and controlled, has endured through the ages, there is no one single body of doctrine, to which the name of Socialism can be exclusively applied, except, of course, in a general and composite sense. But far from this being a paralysing weakness, it only shows the vitality of Socialist thought and its essentially democratic and libertarian message, which has refused the strait-jacket of a rigid and hidebound dogma. It has also continued to grow all the time, and has thrown up variants in different countries, in accordance with the local circumstances.

A review of the various trends is a fascinating study by itself and serves, if anything, to emphasise the numerous common points and the common heritage of Socialist thought. It is best, therefore, to begin one's study of Socialism by making its history the starting point of one's quest.

### HISTORY OF SOCIALISM

THE HISTORY OF SOCIALIST THOUGHT by H. W. Laidler (Constable), 15/-, pp. 713, 1927.

Unquestionably the best book to start with. It is a bird's-eye view of Socialism from its earliest origins to 1927—from the social prophets of the ancient world to the Russian Revolution of 1917 and the post-war Socialist developments. Plato's Republic, More's Utopia, the French Utopian Socialists, Robert Owen, Marxian Socialism, Fabian Socialism, German Social Democracy and Lassalle, Bernstein and Revisionism, Syndicalism, Guild Socialism, Russia to the Bolshevik Revolution, Principles and Tactics of Communism, Recent Developments in Other Countries, Post-war Socialist Thought, The Co-operative Movement, Miscellaneous Socialisms, all pass in review. Contains several illustrations. An indispensable book.

A HISTORY OF SOCIALISM by Sally Graves (Hogarth Press), 3/6, pp. 308, 1939.

A very useful and handy publication, which is also very inexpensive. Provides a good background to the study of Socialism. Starting from the Industrial Revolution it reviews the development of French Socialist thought, Marxism, Social Democracy in Germany and the evolution of the British Labour Party, the War Years (1914-18), the Soviets in Russia, the Civil War in Spain. Two final chapters deal with: Some Other Socialist Patterns and The Crisis in Socialism. A very interesting biographical appendix follows.

A HISTORY OF SOCIALISM by F. S. Markham (A. & C. Black), 7/6, pp. 328, 1930, is another similar book.

A HISTORY OF BRITISH SOCIALISM by Max Beer, (Allen & Unwin), 15/-, pp. 451, First pub. 1919. One volume Ed. 1940.

"The most complete account of the development of Socialist thought in Great Britain which has yet appeared....the particular aspect of thought with which it is primarily concerned is the effort, partly critical, partly constructive, at once inspiration, theory, prophecy and programme, which had as its object to substitute for the direction of industry by the motive of personal profit and the method of unrestricted competition some principle of organisation more compatible with social solidarity and economic freedom."—From the Introduction by Prof. R. H. Tawney.

---

## THEORY OF SOCIALISM

---

On the Theory of Socialism, as on almost every aspect of the Socialist Movement, there is a vast literature. The following section represents a list of books intended to explain to the general reader, the fundamental principles of Socialism in simple language. And having provided the background lead the reader on, step by step, to a fuller and more detailed study of the different aspects of Socialist theory, the classics of Marxism and the great Labour Movement in its various ramifications.

SOCIALISM, UTOPIAN AND SCIENTIFIC by Frederick Engels, (Allen & Unwin), 3/6.

THE SIMPLE CASE FOR SOCIALISM by G. D. H. Cole, (Gollancz), 5/-.

EVERYBODY'S POLITICAL WHAT'S WHAT by Bernard Shaw, (Constable), 10/-.

THE INTELLIGENT WOMAN'S GUIDE TO CAPITALISM AND SOCIALISM by Bernard Shaw, 2 vols., (Penguin), 9d. each.

DECAY OF CAPITALIST CIVILISATION by Sidney & Beatrice Webb, (Allen & Unwin), 3/6.

PRINCIPLES OF SOCIAL RECONSTRUCTION by Bertrand Russell (Allen & Unwin), 3/6.

PROSPECTS OF INDUSTRIAL CIVILISATION by Bertrand Russell, (Allen & Unwin), 3/6.

EQUALITY by R. H. Tawney, (Allen & Unwin), 4/6.

AQUISITIVE SOCIETY by R. H. Tawney (Bell), 4/6.

POLITICS OF DEMOCRATIC SOCIALISM by E. F. M. Durbin, (Metheun), 8/6.

THE SOCIALIST CASE by Douglas Jay (Labour Book Service), 2/6.

WHY THIS SOCIALISM? by Sir Stafford Cripps, (Gollancz), 2/6.

THE MODERN CASE FOR SOCIALISM by A. W. Humphrey, (Allen & Unwin), 12/6.

CAPITALISM, SOCIALISM AND DEMOCRACY by J. A. Schumpeter, (Allen & Unwin), 15/-.

THE THEORY AND PRACTICE OF SOCIALISM by John Strachey, (Gollancz), 10/6.

WHAT IS OUR DESTINY? by Norman Thomas, (Doubleday Doran), $2.

---

## MARX AND ENGELS

---

Differing schools of Socialist thought have drawn inspiration from the great contribution of Marx and Engels. A popular introduction is *Life and Teachings of Karl Marx* by Max Beer, (Allen & Unwin), 3/6. Before turning to their major works it will be best to go through *The Communist Manifesto* by Marx & Engels (1848), 3d., *Wage Labour and Capital* (1849) 4d. and *Value, Price & Profit* (1865) 1/-, both by Marx. His most important work is:

### DAS KAPITAL

CAPITAL by Karl Marx (Kerr) 3 vols., 12/6 each.

Even among the limited number who explore the riches of Marx's *Capital*, most do not usually go beyond volume I. *Capitalist Production* (1867). This is available in several editions, the most convenient being in the Everyman's Library: *Capital*, 2 vols., 3/- each. It is interesting to note that during the lifetime of Marx only the first volume was published. Volume II

*Capitalist Circulation* and Volume III, *Capitalist Production As A Whole,* were edited and printed by Engels after the death of Marx. The material for the Second Volume was reasonably complete, but the Third volume had to be very painstakingly assembled and pieced together from many writings, written at different times. Engels' devotion and industry are without parallel in literary annals. Volume IV was edited by Karl Kautsky in German, but has not still been translated into English. Reading these three volumes of *Capital* is no easy task and will call for much patience and concentrated study. This is particularly true of volumes II and III. For those who may wish to follow the line of least resistance there are three books that attempt a simplified summary, of these all important but rather complex books.

KARL MARX'S CAPITAL by A. D. Lindsay (Oxford) 3/6.

CAPITAL Abridged & Edited by John Strachey (Kitabistan) Rs. 3/-, pp. 352, 1943.

THE STUDENT'S MARX by E. Aveling (Allen & Unwin) 2/6, pp. 192, Reprint 1942.

Next *Anti-Duhring* by F. Engels (Lawrence & Wishart) 5/-, pp. 364. It is a spirited attack on the theory of Socialism propounded by Herr Eugene Duhring. *Socialism Utopian & Scientific* is a part of this larger book.

## *EXPLAINING MARX AND ENGELS*

There are many books seeking to explain Marx: *The Teachings of Karl Marx* by Lenin, *What Marx Really* Meant by G. D. H. Cole, and *Towards the Understanding of Karl Marx* by Sidney Hook are three. *An Essay On Marxian Economics* by Joan Robinson is another stimulating study. Standard lives are *Karl Marx* by Franz Mehring and *Frederich Engels* by J. P. Meyer. Two other stimulating studies are by D. Ryazanoff: *Karl Marx and Frederich Engels* and *Karl Marx, Man, Thinker and Revolutionist,* the latter a symposium.

## CRITICISM

There is a large volume of literature critical of Marxian theories. Since the publication in 1909 of Bernstein's *Evolutionary Socialism* a whole school of thought known as *Revisionism* grew up in Germany, seeking to revise Marx. Friendly but critical comment is offered in *Historical Materialism and the Economics of Karl Marx* by Benedetto Croce and in *Karl Marx* by H. J. Laski. For out and out hostile criticism see *Karl Marx and the Close of His System* by Boehm Bawerk.

## LENIN

Lenin's writings are now available in a Selected Edition of 12 volumes, (Martin Lawrence), 6/6 each. Among his important works are: *The State and the Revolution, Imperialism, Left-Wing Communism: An Infantile Disease,* and *On Religion.* These can be had in a number of inexpensive editions.

---

## UTOPIAN SOCIALISM

---

HISTORY OF UTOPIAN THOUGHT by J. O. Hertzler (Macmillan), 1923.

BREAD AND ROSES: AN UTOPIAN SURVEY AND BLUEPRINT by Ethel Mannin (Macdonald) 10/6, pp. 192, 1944.

LIFE OF ROBERT OWEN by G.D.H. Cole (Macmillan) 5/-.

LOOKING BACKWARD by Edward Bellamy (Foulsham) 4/6-, pp. 188 (many different editions).

Hertzler's book is a mine of information on Utopian Socialism and for the ideas and activities of Owen, Fourrier, St. Simon among others. Ethel Mannin's splendid *Bread & Roses* is a survey of various conceptions of Utopia from Plato to Wells. *Looking Backward* is a famous novel that has influenced the lives of many famous personalities and turned their thoughts towards Socialism. It has sold well near a million and half copies.

## FABIAN SOCIALISM

FABIAN SOCIALISM by G. D. H. Cole (Allen & Unwin) 7/6, pp. 172, 1943.

FABIAN ESSAYS by Bernard Shaw, Sidney Webb, William Clarke, Oliver, Graham Wallas and Annie Besant (Fabian Society), 3/6, 1920.

FABIAN TRACTS (Fabian Society) 12/6, pp. 1641, 1884 to 1931.

The Fabian Socialists emphasise, in the classic words of the Webbs, "the gradual substitution of organised co-operation for the anarchy of competitive struggle" and "the inevitability of gradualness". According to them Socialism must be (1) Democratic, and thus acceptable to the mass of the people, (2) gradual, and thus causing no dislocation, (3) not regarded as immoral by the people, (4) constitutional and peaceful.

## SYNDICALISM

ROADS TO FREEDOM by Bertrand Russell (Allen & Unwin) 3/6, 1923.

SYNDICALISM IN FRANCE by Louis Levine (P. S. King) 7/6, 1914.

REFLECTIONS ON VIOLENCE by G. Sorel (Allen & Unwin) 7/6, 1916.

SYNDICALISM by J. Ramsay MacDonald, (Constable), 3/6, 1912. (Critical).

ANARCHO-SYNDICALISM by Rudolf Rocker, (Secker & Warburg) 3/6, 1938.

Syndicalism relies on *industrial* as opposed to *political* action to bring about the revolutionary transformation of society. It distrusts political action in fact and calls for the abolition of the political state. In its new industrial structure the *Producer* and not the *Consumer* will be the guiding and controlling factor. It regards Syndicates (Trade Unions) alone as the proper instruments of revolution, and the General Strike and other forms of direct action as the means for effecting the emancipation of the people.

---

## ANARCHISM

---

A. B. C. OF ANARCHISM by Alexander Berkman, (Freedom Press, London), 6/-, 1942.

CONQUEST OF BREAD by P. Kropotkin (Vanguard Press, N. Y.), 75 cents.

MUTUAL AID by P. Kropotkin, 1906 (Penguin Books) 9d.

PROPERTY IS THEFT by P. J. Proudhon, (Vanguard Press, N.Y.), 75 cents.

MICHAEL BAKUNIN by E. H. Carr, 25/-, 1937.

PHILOSOPHY OF ANARCHISM by Herbert Read, (Freedom Press) 5/-, 1940.

IMPOSSIBILITIES OF ANARCHISM by Bernard Shaw (Fabian Tracts), 1893.

The Anarchists like the Syndicalists are opposed to the political state in any form, and likewise disdain parliamentary action. They visualise the development of a co-operative industrial commonwealth, loosely federated and completely autonomous, held together on an entirely voluntary basis. There would be no compulsion, no law, no government imposing decisions by force, all acts to spring from the voluntary consent of the community. One school strongly favours the use of force to bring about the revolution, while another section prefers to leave "indiscriminate killing and injuring to the Government, to its statesmen, its stock-brokers, its officers and its law" (*Roads to Freedom* by Bertrand Russell).

Proudhon, Bakunin and Kropotkin are the great leader of Anarchist thought. Karl Marx was on the worst terms possible with Proudhon and Bakunin, both his contemporaries. In his *Poverty of Philosophy* Marx castigates Proudhon in his characteristic style:

"M. Proudhon has the misfortune of being peculiarly misunderstood in Europe. In France, he has the right to be a bad economist, because he is reputed to be a good German philosopher. In Germany, he has the right to be a bad philosopher, because he is reputed to be one of the ablest of French economists. Being both German and economist at the same time, we desire to protest against this double error." (p. 25).

## GUILD SOCIALISM

ROADS TO FREEDOM by Bertrand Russell (Allen & Unwin) 3/6, 1923.

NATIONAL GUILDS AND THE STATE by S. G. Hobson (Macmillan), 1919.

GUILD SOCIALISM RESTATED by G. D. H. Cole (Parsons), 6/-, 1920.

AN ALPHABET OF ECONOMICS by A. R. Orage, (T. Fisher Unwin), 1917.

ECONOMIC DEMOCRACY by Major C. H. Douglas.

Guild Socialism aims at a social order half way between Syndicalism and Socialism. It stresses the importance of the functional principle both in industry and politics, and insists that industrial control should rest in the hands of the workers who perform the tasks and not in those of functionless owners. By workers is meant *all* the workers in an industry, trade or profession, not only the manual workers, but the technical and managerial staff as well. Developing the idea of self-government in industry, it warns against the dangers of an omnipotent State and its bureaucratic collectivism. The chief protagonists of Guild Socialism have been A. J. Penty, A. R. Orage, S.G. Hobson and G. D. H. Cole. It has noticeably influenced Socialist thinking.

## SINGLE TAX

PROGRESS AND POVERTY by Henry George (Vanguard Pr., N.Y.), 75 cents, 1879.

A book that has had great influence. Bernard Shaw declared that it helped to convert him to Socialism. It is a plea for a Single-Tax on land. Land, Henry George argues, is by natural right the common property of mankind. Consequently rent is unearned increment and should be socialised. He favours leaving the land in private hands and taxing all the unearned increment, to be devoted to the welfare of society.

## COMMUNISM

COMMUNISM by Ralph Fox. (Bodley Head), 3/6, pp. 156, 1935.

DIALECTICS by T. A. Jackson (Lawrence & Wishart) 12/6.

A HISTORY OF BOLSHEVISM by A. Rosenberg, (Oxford), 5/-, pp. 250, 1934.

COMMUNISM by H. J. Laski, (Home Univ. Library), 3/-, pp. 254, 1927. (Critical).

LABOUR REVOLUTION by Karl Kautsky, (Critical).

THE BETRAYAL OF THE LEFT by Victor Gollancz, John Strachey and others (Gollancz) 9/-, 1940.

Explain the principles and tactics of the Communists. The controversy between the Communists and other schools of Socialists is well-known. These books help to throw light on it.

Apart from these, the books under the headings, *History of Socialism, Marx & Engels* and *The Internationals*, should be particularly consulted.

## TROTSKYISM

PERMANENT REVOLUTION by Leon Trotsky, (Pioneer Publishers) $2, pp. 157, 1931.

CONQUEST OF POWER by Albert Weisbord (Secker & Warburg) 2 Vols., 25/-, pp. 1208.

A HISTORY OF AMERICAN TROTSKYISM by James P. Cannon (Pioneer Publishers) $2.75, pp. 280, 1943.

Trotsky attacks the Theory of Socialism-In-One-Country advanced by Stalin and against it puts forward his Theory of Permanent Revolution. *Conquest of Power* is a comprehensive review and critique of the entire social theory—Liberalism, Anarchism, Syndicalism, Socialism, Fascism and Communism—generally from the Trotskyite angle.

## MANAGERIAL REVOLUTION

THE MANAGERIAL REVOLUTION by James Burnham, (Putnam), 7/6, 1943. (Penguin), 9d. 1944.

THE MACHIEAVILLIANS by James Burnham (Putnam), 7/6, pp. 202, 1943.

In the long conflict between Capitalism and Socialism the former has been worsted. But Socialism, says Burnham, has not occupied the breach, for what has come instead has not been a Socialist but a Managerial Revolution. The managers and the officials have seized power and brought into being the all-powerful Totalitarian State, riding roughshod over both liberty and democracy. This is the thesis of Burnham. In *The Machiavellians,* he examines the philosophies of Mosca, Sorel, Michels and Pareto and tries to elucidate as to how far the Machiavellian tradition can be a guide to politics in the present-day world.

## THE INTERNATIONALS

HISTORY OF THE FIRST INTERNATIONAL by G. M. Stekloff, (Lawrence), 10/6, pp. 418, 1928.

THE WORKERS' INTERNATIONAL by R. W. Postgate (Swarthmore Press), 3/6, pp. 125, 1920.

The first two Internationals and a short sketch of the origins of the Third, which had come into existence only the previous year in 1919.

THE TWO INTERNATIONALS by R. Palme Dutt (Allen & Unwin) pp. 92, 1920.

Deal with the "collapse" of the Second and the foundation of the Third.

THE MANIFESTO OF THE THIRD INTERNATIONAL signed by Lenin, Trotsky, Platten, Zinoviev and Rakovsky (Text given in *Bolshevik Theory* by R. W. Postgate as also in Palme Dutt).

REPORTS OF THE VARIOUS CONGRESSES OF THE THIRD INTERNATIONAL.

THE COMMUNIST INTERNATIONAL by F. Borkenau (Faber), 10/6, pp. 442, 1938.

A critical survey of the Third International by an ex-member of its Executive.

WORLD REVOLUTION 1917-1936: THE RISE AND FALL OF THE COMMUNIST INTERNATIONAL by C. L. R. James (Secker & Warburg) 12/6, pp. 429,

1937. A critical account by another ex-member of the Executive of the Comintern.

THE THIRD INTERNATIONAL AFTER LENIN by Leon Trotsky (Pioneer Publishers), $3, pp. 357, 1936.

FOUNDING CONFERENCE OF THE FOURTH INTERNATIONAL (Pioneer Publishers) 25 cents. pp. 127.

# CAPITALISM

## CASE FOR CAPITALISM

THE CASE FOR CAPITALISM by Hartley Withers (Eveleigh Nash), 6/-, 1920.

The case for capitalism presented with brilliance and much painstaking argument, by the author of *Meaning of Money, Lombard Street* and other well-known works. An attack on Socialism, the writer arguing that Capitalism having created the modern world must be continued in the interests of progress with its admitted defects removed.

THE AGE OF FABLE by Dr. Gustav Stoper ((Harrap), 10/6, pp. 318, 1943.

An erudite and provocative study of a world that has 'gone to pieces', its standards, its beliefs, and its assumptions, and a plea for a liberal capitalism. A vigorous attack on current 'fables', such as the 'fables' of 'Collectivist Utopia', 'Capitalist Chaos', 'Soviet Planning', 'Production for Profit versus Production for Use', 'Decadent Democracies', etc. Incidentally the author is quite impressed with British achievements in India!

Also consult: *Capitalism and Its Culture* by J. Davis, and *Capitalism—The Creator: Economic Foundations of Modern Industrial Society* by Carl Snyder (Macmillan) 16/-, 1940.

## EVOLUTION OF CAPITALISM

THE EVOLUTION OF MODERN CAPITALISM by J. A. Hobson (Allen & Unwin), 7/6, pp. 510, 1894. 8th Reprint 1928. pp. 510.

A comprehensive and scholarly work which treats of the rise of modern Capitalism. It belongs to that category of authoritative background books which, even if they are not very easy to read, must be read.

## FINANCE CAPITALISM

**THE EVOLUTION OF FINANCE CAPITALISM** by G. W. Edwards, (Longmans), 18/-, pp. 429, 1938.

An examination of the growth of Security Capitalism in England, France, Germany, Italy, Russia, Japan and particularly in the U.S.A.—from the close of the Napoleonic wars to the present day (1820-1935). The author emphasises how the institutions of finance have come to dominate the economic system. He discusses such subjects as the expansion of capital, the increase of security investment, the rise of public debt, the huge expenditure on armaments and wars, inflation and monetary manipulation, and the relation of savings to investment. Ten appendices furnish statistical data for a closer study of the evolution of Security Capitalism, and there are 42 further tables. The author who is the Head of the Department of Economics at the College of the City of New York has spent 15 years on this study. It is claimed on his behalf that the book "can be expected to do for the capitalist system what *Das Kapital* did for the Marxian doctrine."

Two very interesting pamphlets: *Incentives Under Capitalism and Socialism* by H. W. Laidler, 15 cents. pp. 54, 1933, and *Poor Old Competition* by Stuart Chase 10 Cents, pp. 36, 1931, both published by the League of Industrial Democracy, New York, deserve to be widely known. *Decline of Competition* by A. R. Burns (1936) is a more comprehensive work.

## TRUSTS AND CARTELS

For the rise of giant trusts and cartels *International Combines in Modern Industry* by Alfred Plummer (1934) is important. A useful pamphlet is *Monopoly and Big Business* by I. Lipkowitz, (L.I.D.), 20 cents. pp. 56. 140. Other interesting studies are *Big Business: Its Growth And Place* (Twentieth Century Fund) (1939), *Cartels, Combines and Trusts in Post-war Germany* by R. K. Michels, *Concentration of Control in American Industry* by Dr. H. W. Laidler (Crowell) $3.75, 1931 and *Cartels: Challenge to a Free World* by W. Berge, the present Asst. Attorney-General of the U.S.A. (Public Affairs Press), $3.25, 1944.

Consult also the section of Imperialism.

*The Story of the Great American Fortunes* by G. Myers (Modern Library Giants) $1.45, and *Robber Barons* by Mathew Josephson (Harcourt) $3, 1934, are tell-tale books that show how the great fortunes of the modern money barons were made.

## POVERTY AND PLENTY

For a criticism of Capitalism from the 'Poverty-in-the-midst-of plenty' angle see *Poverty in Plenty* by J. A. Hobson (Gollancz) 2/6, and three books by the well-known American economist, Stuart Chase: *The Economy of Abundance, Tragedy of Waste* and *Idle Men, Idle Money.*

## THE NEW DEAL

Another school of thinkers who have lost faith in Capitalism, are now seeking a new middle way. One of their most brilliant spokesmen is Thurman Arnold, whose *Folklore of American Capitalism* (Yale Univ. Press), \$3, pp. 400, 1937, created quite a flutter. It is a slashing attack on Capitalism and its inadequacies. He is for neither Capitalism nor Socialism, but a new type of American radicalism.

Quite a number of this school have seen in President Roosevelt's 'New Deal' the new approximation and the way out. See *The Roosevelt Revolution* by E. K. Lindlay (Gollancz) 5/-, 1934. *The History of the New Deal* by Basil Rauch (Creative Age Press) \$2.50, 1944. Also Henry A. Wallace's *The Century of the Common Man,* \$1.50, 1943 and *Democracy Reborn,* \$3, 1944 (both Reynal and Hitchkock). A critical reply to this view point is given in *After the New Deal—What?* by Norman Thomas, President of the Socialist Party of America (Macmillan) \$2, 1936, who argues that planning under Capitalism is not possible.

---

## CAPITALISM AND WAR

---

For the connection between the giant armament combines and War a great volume of evidence is now available. *Death Pays A Dividend* (*Arms Traffic*) by Fenner Brockway & F. Mullally (Gollancz) 1944, *Merchants of* Death by H. C. Englebrecht, 3/6, 1934, and *Private Manufacture of Armaments* by P. Noel Baker, (Gollancz) 2 Vols., 18/- each, 1936-37 show with unimpeachable documentation, how the Armament Industry, run for private profit, under capitalist management, serves as a great incentive to war. The activities of Armstrong-Vickers, Schneider-Creusot, Krupps, Skoda, Boeing—and others and the adventures of armament kings like Sir Basil Zaharoff, make significant reading. (*Zaharoff* by R. Neumann 1935).

A well-documented account of how Allied Big Business sold arms and armament secrets to Germany and Japan is given in *Patents For Hitler: The Stranglehold of*

*International Cartels* by Guenther Reimann (Gollancz) 6/- 1945.

The Oil Industry similarly has been the subject of widespread investigation. *Oil Imperialism: The International Struggle for Petroleum* by Louis Fischer (International Publishers) pp. 256, 1926, *We Fight For Oil* by Ludewell Denny (Knopf) $3, pp. 297, 1930, and *Oil: An International Study* (Foreign Policy Association) 25 cents, 1942, underline the same argument.

Two other books which seek to show that in the modern world the voice is the voice of politicians but the hand is the hand of money, are *Profits and Politics in the Post-War World* by R. D. Charques & A. H. Ewer (Gollancz), 5/-, pp. 288, 1934, and *Property or Peace* by H. N. Brailsford, (Gollancz), 3/6, 1934.

## CAPITALISM AND PLANNING

This brings up the whole question of planning. Is planning desirable? Is it compatible with a democratic society? Prof. F. A. Hayek, one of the most erudite economists of the Capitalist school, in his *Road to Serfdom* (Routledge) 5/- 1944, discusses the nature and consequences of planning and comes to the conclusion that planning leads to the Totalitarian State and so to servitude. In an earlier study, a symposium, "*Collectivist Economic Planning* (Routledge) 12/6, pp. 293, 1938, a group of eminent continental economists, including Pearson, Mises, Holm, Baron and Hayek offer similar strong criticism. In a recent Fabian Society symposium *Can Planning Be Democratic?* (Vora: Bombay) Rs. 2/-, 1944, Herbert Morrison, T. W. Agar, Barbara Wooton, C. E. M. Joad, Joan Robinson, and G. D. H. Cole do not give a categorical reply, but seem inclined to think that with suitable precautions, it can be. *Plan or No Plan* by Barbara Wooton (Gollancz), 5/-, pp. 360, 1934, is a constructive study of two opposing economic systems and designed to show why the planned society is vastly superior. *Moscow Has A Plan* by M. Ilin (Cape) 3/6, pp. 218, 1931, is a delightful book on the Russian Five Year Plan. There are several other reports on the Russian Plans.

Following the publication of *A Plan For the Economic Development for India* (New Book Co., Bombay) 2 Parts Re. 1/- each, by eight leading Indian Industrialists, various other similar schemes have been published in India also, especially the *Gandhian Plan* by S. N. Agarwal.

## CAPITALISM AND DEMOCRACY

An important study that raises such questions as Can Capitalism Survive? Can Socialism Work? What is the relation between Democracy and Capitalism and Democracy and Socialism? is *Capitalism, Socialism and Democracy* by J. A. Schumpeter (Allen & Unwin) 15/-, pp. 381, 1943. The author, who is a Professor at Harvard University, and who writes as a non-party, unorthodox Socialist, makes a survey of Marxian doctrine and of Marx in the role of prophet, sociologist, economist and teacher. The last seventy-five pages give a historical sketch of Socialist parties from the Nonage to the Second World War.

*It is Later Than You Think: The Need For A Militant Democracy* (Chambers), 12/6, pp. 260, 1939, and *Ideas Are Weapons,* (Viking Press N.Y.) $3, pp. 553, 1939 both by Professor Max Lerner are two other thought-provoking studies. The author himself summarises his arguments for us:

> 'The great political battle of our generation is the battle over what democracy means and how it can survive. The great political task of our generation is the task of giving economic content to democracy and of keeping power in a collectivism from becoming tyrannical........of making democracy militant enough and collectivism democratic enough to sur-

vive . . . And if there is any sense of urgency, it is because for starting vigorously. It is later than you think.' (Foreword). *Ideas Are Weapons,* a collection of the author's essays and reviews, brilliantly elaborates the same arguments.

# FASCISM

"Fascism", Mr. John Strachey has it, "denies every one of the assumptions upon which the progressive movement is based. Fascism proclaims that the whole great hope, by the light of which the peoples of the West have lived for a century, is a great illusion; that democracy is a decaying corpse; international peace, a coward's dream; equality of opportunity, a chimera; the conquest of poverty, a futile vision." (*Menace of Fascism,* p. 42).

## GENERAL

DICTATORSHIP: ITS HISTORY AND THEORY by A. Cobban (Cape), 12/6, pp. 352, Revised 1943.
Dictatorship under a searchlight. A competent survey, partly historical, partly analytical.

THE PSYCHOLOGY OF FASCISM by Peter Nathan (Faber), 8/6, pp. 157, 1943.
A brilliant and stimulating book. A psychological approach to Fascism, concerned not so much with its economic aspects as with the human side. The chapter headings give a good insight into the book: On the Acceptance of Government, Projection, The Frightened Male, The Leader Principle, Fascism Makes You Feel Good, The Desire For Aggression, Germany and the Future.

## PRO-FASCIST

THE POLITICAL AND SOCIAL DOCTRINES OF FASCISM by Benito Mussolini (Hogarth Press), 1/-, pp. 26, 1933.

A panegyric on Fascism, from its most illustrious exponent. Originally contributed as an article to the *Encyclopaedia Italiana.*

WHAT IS FASCISM AND WHY? Edited by G. Silani, 15/-.

A semi-official publication that explains the tenets of Italian Fascism, and endeavours to show as to how it was in the national tradition.

FASCISM by J.T.S. Barnes (Home Univ. Library), 3/-, pp. 2551, 1931.

A sympathetic account of Fascism by an English writer many years resident in Italy.

---

## ANTI-FASCIST

---

FASCISM AND SOCIAL REVOLUTION by R. Palme Dutt (Lawrence), 2/6, pp. 296, 1934.

An able survey by a well-known Communist theoretician.

THE NAZI DICTATORSHIP by F. L. Schumann, (Knopf), $3.50, pp. 516, 1935, Revised 1939.

A comprehensive and definite analysis of both the National Socialist movement and the new Nazi State. Full and critical treatment of the organisation, philosophy and strategy of the Nazi Party.

THE FASCIST: HIS STATE AND HIS MIND by E.B. Ashton (William Morrow), 6/-, pp. 320, 1937.

THE MENACE OF FASCISM by John Strachey (Gollancz), 5/-, 1934.

FASCISM AND BIG BUSINESS by Daniel Guerin (Pioneer Pub.) $1, pp. 376, 1938.

UNDER THE AXE OF FASCISM by G. Salvemini (Gollancz), 7/6, pp. 445, 1936.

GOLIATH: THE MARCH OF FASCISM by G. A. Borgese (Gollancz), 16/-, 1937.

THE FRUITS OF FASCISM by Herbert L. Matthews (Harcourt Brace), $3, 1943.

# IMPERIALISM

It was Lenin who popularised the description of Imperialism as 'the last stage of Capitalism' and 'the characteristic feature of our era'. It is not possible to understand the world today without a proper understanding of the sinister workings of Imperialism.

OUTLINE OF MODERN IMPERIALISM by The Plebs League (National Council of Labour Colleges), 3/6.
A thought-provoking little book dealing with the theory of Imperialism.

WHY WERE THEY PROUD? A STUDY OF EMPIRE (Pacifist Research Bureau) 1/-, pp. 143, 1938.
A good introduction. Pioneers of Modern Imperialism, Scramble for Africa, The Mandates System, Post-Colonial Policy, Conditions of the Subject Peoples, are some of the topics dealt with.

THE FOUNDATIONS OF IMPERIALIST POLICY by M. Pavlovitch (Labour Pub. Co.) 3/6, pp. 159, 1922.
The theory of Imperialism dealt with in six lectures.

IMPERIALISM: A STUDY by J. A. Hobson (Constable) pp. 331, 1905, 3rd. Ed., 8/6, 1938.
A standard work. Contains a discussion of the general principles which underlie Imperialist policy, with special reference to the working of British Imperialism. Part One deals with the "Economics of Imperialism" and Part Two with the "Politics of Imperialism."

IMPERIALISM by V. I. Lenin (Vanguard Pr.) N. Y., 75 cents. pp. 108, 1917.
In this essay the world's great revolutionist examines the economic nature of Imperialism. It was written in 1916, when its author was in exile in Switzerland.

IMPERIALISM AND WORLD POLITICS by P. T. Moon. (Macmillan), 15/-, pp. 583, 1926. A remarkable study of the economic and social forces behind international diplomacy. It places in perspective the working of Imperialism all the world over. In the words of Prof. Moon: "Throughout the book, it is to be hoped, the reader will see the exporter, the factory owner, the concession hunter, the missionary, the admiral, peering over the shoulders of the diplomat." (viii). There are 16 maps.

THE BALANCE SHEET OF IMPERIALISM by Grover Clark (Columbia Univ. Pr.) $3.50, 1936.

"Three main claims have been made as to the value of colonies; that they provide important outlets for population; that the possession of them gave important opportunities for profitable trade, which otherwise would not be available; that control over the source of raw materials in colonies added to a nation's security in times of war, and gave it important advantages in times of peace. The actual records of the colonies, especially for the past half century, when the taking and administering of colonies has gone on under modern conditions, demonstrates conclusively that each of the three claims is essentially falacious".

INTERNATIONAL COMBINES IN MODERN INDUSTRY by Alfred Plummer, 1934.

EMPIRE by Louis Fischer (John Day) $1, 1943.

IMPERIALISM UNMASKED by Louis Fischer (Hamara Hindustan Pub., Bombay) Annas 8/-, pp. 55, 1943.

THE WAR OF STEEL AND GOLD by H. N. Brailsford (Bell), 3/6, pp. 340, 1914.

DOLLAR DIPLOMACY by Scott Nearing & Joseph Freeman (Viking Pr., N.Y.), 1926.

DIPLOMACY OF IMPERIALISM by W. L. Langer (Knopf, N.Y.), 2 Vols., pp. 819, 1935.

THE COLONIAL PROBLEM (Royal Inst. of Int. Affairs), 21/-, pp. 462, 1937.

THE COLONIAL PROBLEM: RAW MATERIALS AND COLONIES (Royal Inst. of Int. Affairs) 1936.

THE FUTURE OF COLONIAL PEOPLES by Lord Hailey (Royal Inst. of Int. Affairs), 3/6, 1943.

THE FRENCH COLONIES: PAST AND FUTURE by Jacques Stern (Didier, N. Y.), $3, pp. 352, 1944, 10 Maps.

THE COLONIAL PROBLEM AND THE FEDERAL SOLUTION by Norman Bentwich, (Macmillan), 6d., 1941.

THE CLAMOUR FOR COLONIES by H. S. Ashton, (Butterworth), pp. 192, 1936.

INDIAN SHIPPING: A Case Study In the Working of Imperialism by Ashoka Mehta (Kitabistan, Allahabad) Re. 1/-, pp. 110, 1940.

BLACK MAN'S BURDEN by E. D. Morel, (National Labour Pr.) 3/6, 1920.

EMPIRE AND COMMERCE IN AFRICA by L. S. Woolf (Labour Pub. C.) 21/-, 1929.

WHITE CAPITAL AND COLOURED LABOUR by Lord Oliver, 1929.

WARNING FROM THE WEST INDIES by W. M. Macmillan (1936) Penguin, 9d.

A HISTORY OF NATIONALISM IN THE EAST by Hans Kohn (Routledge), 25/-, 1929.

THE DUTY OF EMPIRE by Leonard Barnes, (Gollancz), 10/6, pp. 310, 1935.

WE FIGHT FOR OIL by Ludwell Denny (Knopf, N.Y.) $3, pp. 297, 1928.

AMERICA CONQUERS BRITAIN by Ludwell Denny, (Allen & Unwin), 12/6, 1930.

# NATIONALISM

NATIONALISM (Royal Inst. of Int. Affairs), 12/6, pp. 380, 1939.

A valuable contribution to the problem by a study group of the Institute.

THE IDEA OF NATIONALISM by Hans Kohn (Macmillan) $7.50, pp. 722, 1944.

Able, scholarly, yet very readable. Gives the story of the progress of civilisation, with the idea of nationalism as the background. It traces the development of nationalism through recorded history, among the ancient Hebrews and the Arabs, the Greeks and the Romans, the Middle Ages, through the Renaissance to the Nation States of 18th and 19th century Europe and finally America. Germany comes in for detailed treatment. The notes alone occupy 150 pages.

NATIONALISM IN HISTORY AND POLITICS by F. Hertz (Kegan Paul), 25/-, pp. 417, 1944.

A study of the social background of modern nationalism. Taking the Middle Ages as his starting point, the author examines the influence of the doctrines of well-known social philosophers on the nationalist ideology of principal nations. This he does by investigating the relationship between national consciousness and such factors as race, language, religion, territory and state. An extremely stimulating and enjoyable book.

NATIONAL SELF-DETERMINATION by Alfred Cobban (Roy. Inst. of Int. Affairs), (Oxford), 15/-, pp. 186, 1945.

A refreshing analysis of the theory and practice of National Self-Determination; the problems raised by the claims of National Sovereignty and how they stand in relation to the dominant economic and strategic factors; and finally their bearing on world peace and progress.

## FOR FURTHER STUDY

THE WORLD OF NATIONS, A STUDY OF THE NATIONAL IMPLICATIONS IN THE WORK OF KARL MARX by S. F. Bloom 1941.

ON THE RIGHT OF NATIONS TO SELF-DETERMINATION by Lenin (1914) in *Lenin's Selected Works* Vol. IV (Martin Lawrence), 6/6.

THE SOCIALIST REVOLUTION AND THE RIGHT OF NATIONS TO SELF-DETERMINATION by Lenin (1916) in *Lenin's Selected Works*. Vol. 5, (Martin Lawrence), 6/6.

MARXISM AND THE NATIONAL COLONIAL QUESTION by J. Stalin, (Martin & Lawrence) 10/6.

ESSAYS IN NATIONALISM by Carleton Hayes (Macmillan), 12/6, 1926.

THE HISTORICAL EVOLUTION OF MODERN NATIONALISM by Carleton Hayes (Smith) $5, 1931.

A HISTORY OF NATIONALISM IN THE EAST by Hans Kohn (Routledge), 25/-, pp. 476, 1939.

A HISTORY OF NATIONALISM IN THE HITHER EAST by Hans Kohn (Routledge), 15/-, pp. 339, 1929.

NATIONALISM IN THE SOVIET UNION by Hans Kohn (Routledge) 12/6, 1933.

GOVERNMENT AND NATIONALISM IN SOUTH EAST ASIA by R. Emerson, L. A. Mills and V. Thompson, (Oxford), 1942.

REVOLT OF ASIA by Upton Close (Putnams), 10/6, pp. 325, 1927.

# PEACE AND WAR

## PEACEFUL CHANGE

Mahatma Gandhi's advocacy and use of the weapon of non-violent resistance for achieving large-scale political and social change has attracted to the subject, world-wide attention and an ever-increasing number of writers.

Gandhiji's own writings on the subject have been assembled in his *Non-Violence in Peace and War* Rs. 7/-, pp. 608, 1944. His *Satyagraha in South Africa*, Rs. 4/- 1928, relates the story of his struggles and victory in the face of overwhelming odds. *Practical Non-Violence* by Kishorilal Mashruwalla, Annas 4/- 1941, is a little tract by one of the most intellectual interpreters of Gandhism in India. Of particular interest are two other studies by Richard B. Gregg, an American writer with first hand knowledge of Indian conditions: *Power of Non-Violence* Rs. 2/-, pp. 398, 1938, and *Discipline For Non-Violence*, annas 4/-, 1941. All these are published by the Navjivan Publishing House, Ahmedabad.

Among other books are: *Ends and Means* by Aldous Huxley (Chatto & Windus) 5/-, pp. 336, 1937, *A History of Peaceful Change in the Modern World* by C. R. M. F. Crutwell (Oxford), 7/6, pp. 230, 1937, *War, Peace and Change* by J. F. Dulles, Foreword by Lionel Curtis (Macmillan), 7/6, 1938, *International Legislation* by T. Gihl (Oxford), 10/6, pp. 166, 1937, *The Conquest of Violence* by Bart de Ligt, *Peaceful Change*, Report of the International Studies Conference, Paris 1938, and *Peaceful Change* by F. S. Dunn (Council on Foreign Relations, N.Y.) 1937. *Plans For World Peace Through Six Centuries* by S. J. Hembleben (Chicago Univ. Pr.) $2.50, pp. 227, 1943, is a history of the projects for universal peace set forth since the early middle ages.

## WAR—IN THEORY AND PRACTICE

"So long", says Liddell Hart, one of Great Britain's foremost authorities on military science, "as force forms the foundation of order between nations and within nations, we are nourishing a delusion when we draw the customary dividing line between war and peace . . . Any study of what are called 'peace' problems, i.e., political and social problems—is not only dependent on our understanding of war, but should start with an understanding of the relation of armed forces to society."

A HISTORY OF MILITARISM by Alfred Vagts (Allen & Unwin), 18/-, pp. 510, 1938, 33 Illustrations.

A comprehensive and scholarly history of militarism from the feudal times to the modern mechanised army. Topics include: From the Mounted Warrior to the Standing Army; American Revolution Challenges the Standing Army; the French Revolution and Napoleon; the Development and Mechanisation of Mass Armies; Philosophy of War in the 19th and 20th Centuries; Military Officers As Politicians; Armies versus Navies; the Theory and Practice of Total Mobilisation for War; Armies and Imperialisms; Post-war Militarisation of Society.

ARMIES AND THE ART OF REVOLUTION by K. C. Chorley (Faber), 12/6, pp. 272, 1943. A notable book. A valuable and objective study dealing with the part that armies have played in various revolutions, both successful as well as unsuccessful.

THOUGHTS ON WAR by Captain B. H. Liddell Hart, (Faber) 12/6, 1944.

A treatise on the nature, conduct and operations of war. A record of conclusions and reflections after a life-time of study, full of epigram and brilliant writing.

THE WAR IN OUTLINE 1914-18 by Captain B. H. Liddell Hart (Modern Library) 95 cents. pp. 285, 1936, Revised 1939.

"The best short history of the war in any language" (*The Listener*).

A MINIATURE HISTORY OF THE WAR by R. C. K. Ensor (Oxford), 2/6, pp. 288, 1944.

A review of the Second World War in a short compass by one of England's leading historians and author of the well-known *England* 1870-1914.

NOTE:—Also consult: *A Study of War* by Quincy Wright; *On War* by Clausewitz; *Victory Through Air Power* by de Seversky; *Sea Power in the Second World War* by Lord Strabolgi; *Blitzkrieg* by F. O. Miksche; *Paratroops* by F. O. Miksche; *Armies on Wheels* by S. L. A. Marshall; *Weapons and Tactics* by Tom Wintringham; *Why Don't We Learn From History?* by B. H. Liddell Hart.

---

## LEAGUE OF NATIONS

---

While the League of Nations must be pronounced a rueful failure, the fault was not with the Idea but the way in which the League machinery was manipulated by the Imperialist powers. The end of the Second World War once again brings to the fore the question of International organisation.

A vast literature exists on the League, its allied organisations and their working. For an understanding of the League its own *Essential Facts About The League of Nations* (Information Department, Geneva) 9th Ed. 1938, is helpful. For a judgment on its work, *A Mirror to Geneva: The League, Its Growth, Grandeur and Decay* by George Slocombe (Cape), 1937, and *A Great Experiment* by Viscount Cecil (Cape) 1941.

The League's impressive volume of publications range over a very wide field, from Health and Nutrition to Education and Disarmament, from simple studies to the most complicated reports. Nearly 200 volumes have been published only in its *Treaty Series*, giving the text of all Treaties made since 1919. Some of its more famous annual publications are: *Statistical Year Book of the League of Nations, The World Economic Survey, The Review of World Trade* and *The Armaments Year Book*. From the International Labour Office likewise come the *I.L.O. Year Book* and *The Year Book of Labour Statistics*.

## MANDATES, PLEBISCITES, SANCTIONS, LEND-LEASE

The following may be consulted as of kindred interest. *Mandates* by F. White (Cape), 5/-, pp. 196, 1926; *International Sanctions* by The Royal Inst. of Int. Affairs, 12/6, pp. 258, 1938; *The Employment of the Plebiscite in the Determination of Sovereignty* by J. Mattern, (1920). *A Monograph On Plebiscites* (1920) and *Plebiscites Since the War* by Sarah Wambaugh, (Carnegie Endowment for World Peace) 1933, a well-known American authority on Plebiscites and author of several studies on the subject. Finally *Report of the Committee for the Study of the Problem of Raw Materials* (League of Nations, Geneva), 1937. For an understanding of the complex mechanism of Lend-Lease, devised during World War II, see *Lend-Lease: Weapon of Victory* by E. R. Stettinus Jr. (Penguin) 9d. 1944, formerly Lend-Lease Administrator and Secretary of State of the U.S.A.

## WORLD RE-ORGANISATION

From the days of Plato the world has not lacked schemes that could carry it right to the heart of Utopia. The Second World War has provided a fresh impetus. In

U.S.A. alone there are no fewer than 47 learned societies, besides quite a number of individuals who have been working on different aspects of post-war reconstruction. So extensive has been their output, that the bibliography itself has needed a volume to itself—*A Survey of Literature on Post-War Reconstruction* by Professor A. Sturmthal (New York University Press), $1, 1943.

Some of the more ambitious works, by thinkers of different countries, and published during the last few years are given here. *The Problem of the Twentieth Century* by Lord David Davies, 1931; *The United States of Europe* by Edouard Herriot, 1930; *The United States of Europe* by Sir Arthur Saltar, 1933; *Union Now* by Clarence Streit, 1938; *World's Design* by Salvador di Madariaga, 1938; *The Coming Future* by Carl Dreher, 1943; *Reflections on the Revolution of Our Time*, by Harold J. Laski, 1943, *Economic Problem of The Peace* by Walter Padley, 1944, *The Yogi And The Commissar* by Arthur Koesther, 1945.

*The San Francisco Conference* by Vera Michaels Dean (Foreign Policy Association Report) 25 cents. July 15, 1945, gives the background and the particulars of the Charter of World Social Security, which has been the target of widespread criticism, especially in Asia.

For text and other relevant material see a very attractively printed booklet *United Nations Charter* (United States Office of War Information, Bombay) pp. 42, Oct. 1945. Gratis.

# THE LABOUR MOVEMENT

Scarcely half a century ago, it was urged by the progressive Victorian Liberals, that a Parliamentary Labour Party in England was unnecessary, since the working class had no reasonable proposal which the middle class could not pass. It was perhaps a shrewd reflection of the fact that the working class had not appreciably evolved beyond the stage of Trade Union consciousness and British Capitalism being still on the upgrade, could make concessions.

The change during the intervening years is striking. Not many years ago a restricted, constitutional, parliamentary Labour Group appeared unnecessary even to sincere radicals; in recent years Labour Governments have held office in quite a number of countries in Europe and outside.

The story of the Trade Union Movement is truly fascinating. The following selection of books are intended as a help to the study, not only of the efforts of the working class at organisation, but also in giving a perspective of the struggle ahead and vision of the final achievement.

## GENERAL

THE ENCYCLOPAEDIA OF THE LABOUR MOVEMENT by H. B. Lees Smith (Caxton). 3 vols., £3/3, pp. Vol. 1, 321; Vol. 2, 319; Vol. 3, 342.
"The Encyclopaedia covers every important subject which is of concern to the Labour Movement. Each subject has, as far as possible, been explained by the chief expert on it, in the country" (Lees Smith). It

includes a Guide to Reading at the end of each volume and a very full index. Also many illustrations. But very much out-of-date.

TRAGEDY OF EUROPEAN LABOUR: 1918-1939 by Adolf Sturmthal (Gollancz), 7/6, pp. 288, 1944.

A stimulating survey of the causes of the decline and fall of European Labour. Subjects discussed include: Why Labour Failed, From Revolutionary Party to Pressure Group, British Labour Blunders Through, German Labour's "Toleration" Policy, The Failure of the French New Deal, Swedish Labour's Success, The Rise of Fascism, The Popular Front, Labour's Road to Munich, Into the Abyss, The Underground Movement. The author, now a professor at Columbia University, was for 12 years on the Secretariat of the Labour and Socialist International.

THE LABOUR PARTY IN TRANSITION: 1931-1938 by Dean E. McHenry (Routledge) 7/6, pp. 320, 1938.

A review of the structure and problems of the British Labour Party and its record since 1931. Chapters: Rise of the Labour Party, The National Party Organisation, The Central Office: Finance, Organisation, Propaganda, Research, International Problems; Local Organisation, Co-operative Party, Leadership, Parliamentary Labour Party, Tactics and Policies, Recent Conflicts Over Policy, Conclusion.

PROBLEMS OF INDUSTRY IN THE EAST by Harold Butler, (International Labour Office, Geneva), 1/6, pp. 74, 1938.

A concise survey of the problems of labour and industrialisation in India, Ceylon, Malaya and Netherlands Indies.

SOCIAL SECURITY Edited by Dr. W. A. Robson (Allen & Unwin), 15/-, 1943.

A valuable symposium. The first part critically reviews the present position of social insurances, pensions, and other benefit schemes and services. The second part outlines a comprehensive plan of reconstruction and practical suggestions for the improvement of the existing machinery.

ORIGIN OF THE INTERNATIONAL LABOUR OFFICE by James T. Shotwell, (Columbia Univ. Pr.) Oxford, 2 Vols., £2/10, pp. 1132, 1934.

THE GENERAL STRIKE by W. H. Crook (Univ. North Carolina Pr.) 27/-, pp. 649, 1931.

NEW TACTICS IN SOCIAL CONFLICT by H. W. Laidler and Norman Thomas (Symposium), (Vanguard Press) 75 cents. pp. 230, 1926.

UNEMPLOYMENT: AN INTERNATIONAL PROBLEM by a Study Group of the Royal Inst. of Int. Affairs (Oxford) 25/- pp. 496, 1935.

UNEMPLOYMENT 1909-1930 by Sir William Beveridge (Longmans), pp. 514, 1930.

FULL EMPLOYMENT IN A FREE SOCIETY by Sir William Beveridge, (Allen and Unwin), 12/6, 1944.

THE WORKER AND THE STATE by F. Tillyard (Routledge), 10/6, pp. 307, 1936.

ORGANISED LABOUR IN FOUR CONTINENTS: 1918-1938, Edited by H. A. Marquand (Longmans), 18/- pp. 518, 1939.

EASTERN INDUSTRIALISATION AND ITS EFFECTS ON THE WEST by G. E. Hubbard (Oxford Univ. Pr.), 18/- pp. 438. New Ed. 1938.

SOCIAL POLICY IN DEPENDENT TERRITORIES (International Labour Office, Montreal) $1.50, pp. 185. 1944.

DEVELOPMENT OF THE LABOUR MOVEMENT IN GREAT BRITAIN, FRANCE AND GERMANY by W. A. McConagha, (Univ. of North Carolina Pr.) $2.50, pp. 212, (Oxford, 11/6.)

LABOUR PARTY IN PERSPECTIVE by Major Clement Attlee (Gollancz), 7/6, pp. 287, 1937.

TRADE UNIONS, THEIR PAST, PRESENT AND FUTURE by W. A. Appleton (Allen & Unwin) 3/6, 1925.

TRADE UNIONISM by C. M. Lloyd, (A. & C. Black), 5/-, pp. 291, 1928.

MODERN TRADE UNIONISM by J. T. Murphy, (Routledge), 5/-, pp. 199, 1935.

TRADE UNIONS FIGHT—FOR WHAT? by Herbert Tracey (Labour Book Service), 3/6, pp. 222, 1940.

BRITISH TRADE UNIONS by Sir Walter Citrine (Collins), 4/6, pp. 48, 1942, Valuable illustrations.

A group of books, concise, well-written and inexpensive, giving both the theoretical and historical development of the Trade Union Movement, drawing mainly upon British experience.

A HISTORY OF TRADE UNIONISM by Sidney & Beatrice Webb (Longmans Green) 21/-, pp. 558, 1894, Revised 1920.

INDUSTRIAL DEMOCRACY by Sidney & Beatrice Webb (Longmans Green) 21/-, pp. 929, 1897. Revised 1920.

Two monumental studies indispensable for every advanced student of the Labour Movement. The Webbs devoted six years to an intensive examination of the whole field of Trade Unionism, during which they examined the constitution and working of almost every Trade Union in the United Kingdom. *A History of Trade Unionism* traces the growth of the movement both industrially and politically. Chapters on: The Origin of Trade Unionism, The Struggle for Existence (1799-1825), The Revolutionary Period (1829-1842), The New Spirit and the New Model (1843-1860), The Junta and Their Allies (1860-1875), Sectional Developments (1863-1885), The Old Unionism and the New (1875-1889), The Trade Union World (1892-1894), Bibliography of 45 pages.

*Industrial Democracy* has three parts. The first deals with Trade Union Structure; the second is a detailed analysis of Trade Union Function—the methods used, the regulations imposed and the policies pursued; the third deals with theory, with such topics as The Verdict of the Economists, The Higgling of the Market, The Economic Characteristics of Trade Unionism, Trade Unions and Democracy. A 23 page supplementary bibliography.

BRITISH TRADE UNIONISM TODAY Edited by G. D. H. Cole (Gollancz), 7/6, pp. 591, 1939.

The most comprehensive study of the British Trade Union Movement since the two studies of the Webbs. Thrity experts have collaborated to make a survey of the whole field, as well as of the principal industries and services. Starting with Trade Union History and passing on to Collective Bargaining, State Action, Structure of the T.U.C., and of the Trade Councils, Trade Unions in Politics, Trade Union Finance, etc. The next 250 pages are devoted to a review of the organisation of the Miners, Railwaymen, Builders, Metal-workers, Shipbuilders, Engineers, Textile, Shops, Agricultural, and Non-Manual Workers, Teachers, Civil Servants, etc. Then Conclusions, and a Summary Guide to Trade Unionism.

TRADE UNION DOCUMENTS compiled and edited by W. Milne Bailey (Bell), 8/6, pp. 552, 1929.

A valuable source book containing 247 documents on different aspects of Trade Unionism. It is divided into four parts, each with a separate introduction. Value, Aspirations and Objects of Trade Unionism (Documents 1 to 25); Structure and Organisation of Trade Unionism (Documents 26 to 94); Functious and Methods of Trade Unionism (Documents 95 to 194); The Place of Trade Unionism in the Community (Documents 195 to 247).

# LABOUR MOVEMENT

## COUNTRY BY COUNTRY

### AFRICA

LABOUR PROBLEMS OF AFRICA by John A. Noon, (University of Pennsylvania Press, U.S.A.) $1.50, 1944.

A brief monograph, being volume 6 in Africa Handbooks, a new series edited by H. A. Wieschhoff.

### CHINA

FACING LABOUR ISSUES IN CHINA by Chuan-Hua Lowe (Allen & Unwin), 7/6, pp. 2-11, 1934.

An examination of the industrial and labour situation in China. A survey of China's economic crisis and the causes of her agricultural disintegration, of the peculiar forms of Chinese labour, Government's policy towards organised labour; study of some Labour Unions; the Labour policy of the Kuomintang; as also a chapter on 'Will Communism Conquer China?'

LIFE AND LABOUR IN CHINA by R. H. Tawney (Allen & Unwin), 7/6, pp. 207, 1932.

A valuable survey of China's economic framework, including both agriculture and industry. A model of compressed information.

### ENGLAND

A SHORT HISTORY OF THE BRITISH WORKING CLASS MOVEMENT: 1798-1927 by G. D. H. Cole, (Allen & Unwin) 12/6, pp. 615, Revised Edition 1932.

A survey of the British Labour Movement, which deals with both the economic and the political side. Very valuable. Originally issued in three volumes, now available in one. For a more detailed account of Labour politics see the same writer's *British Working Class Politics*: 1832-1914 (Routledge) 6/-.

A SHORT HISTORY OF LABOUR CONDITIONS IN GREAT BRITAIN AND THE EMPIRE by J. Kuczynski (Muller), 12/6, 1942.

An account of the development of labour conditions in Britain from 1750 to the present day. Also chapters on India, Canada, Australia, New Zealand, South Africa, etc.

THE CONDITIONS OF THE WORKING CLASS IN 1844 by Frederick Engels (Allen & Unwin) 5/-, pp. 298, 1892, Latest Ed. 1920.

Originally published in Germany in 1845, when Engels was 24 years of age. It was translated in 1885 and published in America. The English edition came in 1892, to which the author contributed a special preface, reviewing in it the developments during the half century that had elapsed since the orignial publication of the book.

NOTE:—The famous triology, *The Town Labourer, The Village Labourer,* and *The Skilled Labourer* by J. L. & Barbara Hammond (Longmans) 6/- each, are masterly descriptions of labour conditions during the Industrial Revolution. They are in inexhaustible mine of information and cover the period upto 1832. Their *Age of Chartists* (Longmans) 12/6, surveys social conditions during the 1830's and 1840's and throws a vivid light on factory towns.

## FRANCE

LABOUR MOVEMENT IN POST-WAR FRANCE by D. J. Saposs (Oxford) 30/-, pp. 526, 1931.

An enumeration of facts as well as an analysis of tendencies. Exhaustive.

## GERMANY

THE TRADE UNION MOVEMENT IN GERMANY, (Int. Federation of Trade Unions) 1/-, 1928.

A brief but informative account. The whole system described here was scrapped on the coming of the Nazis to power.

LABOUR RELATIONS IN REPUBLICAN GERMANY by N. Reich (Oxford), 12/6, pp. 296, 1938.

A SHORT HISTORY OF LABOUR CONDITIONS IN GERMANY UNDER FASCISM by J. Kuczynski (Muller) 9/6, pp. 239, 1944.

A study of Labour in Germany since the advent of the Nazis to power in 1933. The structure and Economic Policy of Nazism is followed by a review of Labour conditions from 1933 to 1943. This is done, both statistically and as it affects the German worker, from childhood to old age, as also under the impact of World War II.

## INDIA

THE INDIAN WORKING CLASS by Prof. Radha Kamal Mukherjee (Hind Kitabs: Bombay), Rs. 12/8, pp. 336, 1945.

A carefully documented study by a well-known economist. Rather heavy reading, but packed full of information.

INDUSTRIAL WORKER IN INDIA by B. Shiv Rao (Allen & Unwin), 10/6.

An able, conscientious and extremely well-written account of the Labour Movement in India, by one who has been prominently associated with it.

INDUSTRIAL LABOUR IN INDIA (International Labour Office) 7/6, pp. 335, 1938.

A valuable study, the best so far. Chapters: Introduction, Nature and Extent of Industrial Employment, Labour Legislation, Industrial Relations, Employment and Unemployment, Health and Safety, Hours of Work, Wages, Standard of Living, Housing and Welfare, Conclusion.

PRINCIPLES AND PROBLEMS OF INDIAN LABOUR LEGISLATION by Dr. Rajini Kanta Das (Univ. of Calcutta Pr.) Rs. 2/8, pp. 281, 1938.

LABOUR LEGISLATION IN INDIAN STATES by Rajani Kanta Das (I.L.O. Geneva) 1938.

INDIAN FACTORY LEGISLATION by Sir Andrew Clow (Govt. of India) 1941.

A HISTORY OF LABOUR LEGISLATION IN INDIA by J. C. Kydd (Longmans) Rs. 8/-, 1920.

Four accounts of Labour legislation in India. Clow's is an interesting exposition from the official Government point of view. Professor Kydd undertook the study at the instance of the well-known Sally Oakes College. Dr. Das's book is the most comprehensive on the subject. Chapters: Historical Background, Legislative Procedure, Fundamental Principles, Principal Problems, Development of Labour Policy, Development of Industrial Labour, Organisation of the State Function, Social Significance, Rise of the Labour Code, Legislation and Society. The Congress Labour Programme is given in the Appendix. His other books are *Factory Legislation in India, Factory Labour in India, Labour Movement in India*, (Walter de Gruyte & Co., Berlin) 5/- each, 1923. *Child Labour In India* (I.L.O.) 1938.

MARITIME LABOUR IN INDIA by Dinker Desai (Servants of India Society, Bombay), Rs. 2/4, pp. 256, 1940.

PLANTATION LABOUR IN INDIA by Dr. Rajani Kanta Das (Modern Review; Calcutta), Rs. 3/-, 1931.

LABOUR IN THE INDIAN COAL INDUSTRY by Bal Raj Seth (Taraporewalla) Rs. 8/-, pp. 308, 1940.

WOMEN IN MINES by Renuka Ray (All India Women's Conference) (Padma Publications) 8 annas, 1945.

DOCK LABOURERS IN BOMBAY by R. P. Cholia, (Longmans) Rs. 4/8, pp. 165, 1941.

A survey of life and labour in a number of vital industries, with a discussion of special problems affecting each.

REPORT OF ROYAL COMMISSION ON INDIAN LABOUR (Govt. of India, Calcutta) pp. 581, 1931.

A very elaborate survey of labour conditions in India. The volume along with those of Evidence, of which there are no less than 11 in 17 parts, are a veritable encyclopaedia on all matters concerning Indian labour. The conclusions are not adequate but the collection of material is impressive.

THE INDIAN PEASANT UPROOTED by Margaret Read. (Longmans) Rs. 1/8.

A sparkling account based on the Report of the Royal Commission on Indian Labour, and intended to be a summary of its conclusions.

---

## FOR FURTHER STUDY

---

For further study consult: *Industrial Labour in India* by Dr. S. G. Panandikar (1933); *Industrial Welfare in India* by P. S. Lokanathan (1929); *State and Industry* (1928) and *Indian Workmen's Compensation Act* (1936) both by Sir A. Clow; *Regulation of Wages and Other Problems of Industrial Labour in India* by D. R. Gadgil (1943); *Labour in Indian Industries* by G. M. Broughton (Lady Chatterji); *Labour in India* by J. H. Kelman (1923); *Factory Labour in the Punjab* (1929) and *Trade Unionism and Labour Disputes in India* (1938) both by Mukhtar Ahmed; *Housing and Labour in Bombay* by E. Burnett Hurst (1925); *Housing Indian Labour* by Kanji Dwarkadas (1945); *Social Insurance Planning in India* by A. N. Agarwala (1944); *The Problem of Sickness Insurance* by V. P. Keni (1943); *Report on Health Insurance for Industrial Workers* by B. P. Adarker (1944).

For the Textile Labour Association, Ahmedabad, the biggest single Trade Union in India, its annual reports may be consulted. Also an article by its Honorary Secretary, Gulzarilal Nanda, on 'A Charter for Labour' in the 75th Birthday Celebration Volume of Mahatma Gandhi (pp. 178 to 189).

*The Labour Gazette* issued monthly by the Bombay Labour Office (Rs. 12/- a year) contains much useful information. Also *Trade Union Record* published by the All-India Trade Union Congress (Rs. 4/-. a year, Bombay).

## ITALY

CAPITAL AND LABOUR UNDER FASCISM by Carmen Haidar (Columbia Univ. Pr., N. Y.) $2.50, 1930.
A careful and well-documented study of the Italian worker in the Fascist State. Shows the progressive deterioration in their standard of living.

## JAPAN

INDUSTRIAL LABOUR IN JAPAN by the International Labour Office (P. S. King) 10/-, 1933.
An exhaustive survey of Japanese Labour conditions issued by the I.L.O.

LABOUR CONDITIONS IN JAPAN by S. Harada (Columbia Univ. Pr., N.Y.) 10/6, pp. 295, 1928.
A survey of labour conditions, wages, cost of living, hours of work, relations between employers and employees, and government attitude towards Labour.

## NEW ZEALAND

SOCIALISM IN NEW ZEALAND by J. A. Lee, (T. Werner Lawrie) 10/6. 1944.
A sympathetic survey dealing with both the political and the industrial fields.

## SWEDEN

THE GOVERNMENT OF LABOUR RELATIONS IN SWEDEN by James J. Robbins (Univ. of North Carolina Pr.) Oxford, 16/-, pp. 380, 1942.
A scholarly and interesting study of labour in Sweden.

## SOVIET RUSSIA

FROM PETER THE GREAT TO LENIN by S. P. Turin (P. S. King) pp. 220, 1935.
'A History of the Russian Labour Movement with Special Reference to Trade Unionism' (Sub-Title).

THE TRADE UNION MOVEMENT IN SOVIET RUSSIA (Int. Labour Office, Geneva) 4/-, pp. 287, 1928.

A careful and comprehensive study. Not up-to-date but valuable.

SOVIET LABOUR AND INDUSTRY by L. E. Hubbard (Macmillan) 15/-, pp. 315, 1942.

A study of Labour and Industry in the Soviet Union by an economist, whose family has settled in Russia for several generations and who is well acquainted with the language and the people. The historical portion, notes on the various Five Year Plans and on Labour legislation are particularly informative.

LIFE IN A SOVIET FACTORY by Lily Korber (John Lane) 5/- (Sympathetic).

SOVIET TRADE UNIONS by Robert Dunn (Vanguard Press) 75 cents. (Out of date but sympathetic).

WORKERS BEFORE AND AFTER LENIN by Manya Gordon.

## U.S.A.

AMERICAN LABOUR by E. Davies (Allen & Unwin) 2/-, pp. 100, 1943.

The best short account of the American Trade Union Movement. Published under the auspices of the Fabian Society, with an introduction by H. J. Laski.

A SHORT HISTORY OF LABOUR CONDITIONS IN THE U.S.A. by J. Kuczynski (Muller) 10/6, pp. 228, 1943.

A survey of American Labour conditions from 1789, divided into: The Period of Primitive Exploitation (1789-1840), The First Golden Age (1840-1860), The Ripe Years of American Capitalism (1860-1900), The Decline of American Capitalism (1900-1940), Conditions Before the War, Labour and the War.

HISTORY OF LABOUR IN THE UNITED STATES Edited by J. Commons (Macmillan) 4 Vols. Vols. 1 to 3, 20/- each, Vol. 4, 22/6.

The first two volumes published in 1918 bring the history up to 1896. The remaining two volumes published in 1935 carry the account to 1932—to the beginning of the New Deal.

'The period of 1896-1932 is treated as a unit, but owing to the greater fulness and complexity of the material, a departure has been made from the method of presentation in Volumes I and II, where the discussions of the working conditions and Labour Legislation was merely incidental to the discussion of the Labour Movement. In the present study, working conditions and Labour Legislation constitute Volume III and Labour Movements Volume IV. (From Preface to Volume III).

ORGANISED LABOUR AND THE NEGRO by H. R. Northrup (Harper), $3.50, 1944.

NOTE:—For the two main labour organisations in the U.S.A. consult: *The American Federation of Labour* by L. Lorwin and *The Story of the C.I.O.* by Benjamin Stolberg. Also *Labour Baron: Portrait of John L. Lewis* by A. Wechsler, former head of the C.I.O.

# THE PEASANT MOVEMENT

The Peasant, it has been said, is the hub of the Indian Revolution. In a country like India, with its 700,000 villages and the overwhelming mass of its people living in rural areas, the study of the Peasant Movement both here and abroad can scarcely be over-estimated. The number of books on what may strictly be called the Peasant Movement are very limited.

NOTE:—For a study of Economics in this special field consult *Principles of Rural Economics* by T. N. Carver, *Economics of Agriculture* by R. L. Cohen, *Economics of Farm Relief* by E. R. A. Seligman, and *Agriculture in Modern Life* by O. E. Baker, R. Borsodi and M. L. Wilson.

## GENERAL

WORLD AGRICULTURE (Royal Inst. of Int. Affairs) (Oxford) 12/6, pp. 295, 1932.

A thorough and painstaking study of the Question by a Study Group of the Royal Institute of International Affairs.

VILLAGE COMMUNITIES IN THE EAST AND WEST by Sir Henry Maine (Murray) 12/-, pp. 413, 1871, Third Edition, 1876.

A course of lectures mainly delivered before the Universities of Oxford and Calcutta. Subjects include: The Western Village Community, The Eastern Village Community, Process of Feudalisation, Early History of Price and Rent, The Effects of Observation of India on Modern European Thought.

AGRARIAN PROBLEMS FROM THE BALTIC TO THE AEGEAN: DISCUSSION OF A PEASANT PROGRAMME (Royal Inst. of Int. Affairs) 3/-, 1944.

A well planned little book outlining the conclusions of group of agrarian experts representing seven countries, 'from the Baltic to the Aegean', viz., Poland, Czechoslovakia, Hungary, Roumania, Yugoslavia, Bulgaria and Greece. They advocate the break up of large landed estates, but insist on peasant proprietorship as an essential pre-requisite for agricultural progress; the creation of a Central Agricultural Bank to finance the farmer, and the importance of the stabilisation of prices and a balance between agriculture and industry.

INDUSTRY AND RURAL LIFE edited by H. Bryant Newbold (Faber) 8/6, pp. 182, 1942.

An extremely well planned report of a conference of experts at Cambridge on such subjects as Agricultural Planning and Policy, Requirements of Decentralised Industry, Social Life in Villages and Small Towns, Rural Land Ownership and Planning, etc.

---

## THE PEASANT MOVEMENT

### COUNTRY BY COUNTRY

---

### CHINA

THE AGRARIAN PROBLEM IN CHINA by Chen Han Seng (One of the studies in *Problems of the Pacific*) (Oxford) 25/-, 1934.

A paper read before the biennial conference of the Institute of Pacific Relations. A very able study in 35 pages.

CHINA BUILDS FOR DEMOCRACY by Nym Wales (Kitabistan) Rs. 5/4. pp. 311. 1942.

The fascinating story of the Chinese Industrial Co-operatives. Foreword by Jawaharlal Nehru.

PEASANT LIFE IN CHINA by Fei Hsiao Tung (Kegan Paul) 15/-, pp. 300, 1939. Revised 1943.

An interesting socio-anthropological study of a Chinese Village, and a picture of day to day life in rural China. Foreword by B. Malinowski.

LAND AND LABOUR IN CHINA by R. H. Tawney (Allen & Unwin), 7/6, pp. 207, 1932.

Probably the best study of the land problem of China by one of the most eminent of English economic historians.

AGRARIAN CHINA: SELECTED SOURCE MATERIALS FROM CHINESE AUTHORS, compiled and translated by the Research Staff of the Institute of Pacific Relations, N. Y. (Allen & Unwin) 10/6, pp. 258, 1939.

A selection of published and unpublished material from Chinese sources. Makes available some of the great mass of the new research of Chinese scholars into the social and economic problem of their country. Some of the topics are: Land Ownership and its concentration in China, Nature of the Present Land Problems, Characteristic Features of Farm Management, Agrarian Policy of the Kuomintang, Trade Capital and Paper Money in Villages, Effects of Commercialisation of Agriculture, The Experiences of a District Director of Co-operatives, Decline of Handicrafts, Peasant Women and Hand Weaving. R. H. Tawney contributes a valuable Introduction.

## DENMARK

DENMARK: THE CO-OPERATIVE WAY by F. C. Howe, (Coward McCann) $2.50, pp. 293, 1936.

A picture of pre-war Denmark, as a co-operative paradise, where 20 per cent of the national revenue was spent on Education and 21 per cent on social services as against only 13 per cent on Defence.

## ENGLAND

HISTORY OF THE ENGLISH AGRICULTURAL LABOURER by W. Hasbach (P. S. King) 12/6, pp. 465, 1908, Reprinted 1920.

THE VILLAGE LABOURER by J. L. & Barbara Hammong (Longmans) 6/-, 1911. Revised 1927.

THE BATTLE OF THE LAND by Dr. N. Gangulee (Lindsay Drummond) 6/-, Revised Ed. 1944.

LAND AND LANDOWNERS (Labour Research Dept., London) 1/-, 1944.

## GERMANY

GERMAN AGRICULTURAL POLICY: 1918-1934 by J. B. Holt (Univ. of North Carolina Pr.) $2.50, pp. 256, 1936.

PEASANT WARS IN GERMANY by F. Engels (Allen & Unwin) 4/6. pp. 190. 1926.

## INDIA

INDIAN RURAL PROBLEM by Sir Manilal Nanavati & Prof. J. J. Anjaria (Indian Society of Agricultural Economics, Bombay) Rs. 8/-, pp. 422, 1944. Reprinted 1945.

The most important single study of the agrarian problem in India. "If it is true to say", say the authors, "'Industrialise or perish', it is equally important also to remember that we have to modernise, rehabilitate, revitalise and rebuild our rural economy in harmony with the needs of economy as a whole." It deals among other topics with: Environment & Resources, Population, Agriculture, Food Supply & Nutrition, Social Services, The Land Problem, Money-Lender Finance and Debt Legislation, Rural Reconstruction Activities, The Role of the Central Government, Reform of the Land System, Surplus Population and Rural Unemployment, Prime Agencies of Reform.

ECONOMICS OF VILLAGE INDUSTRIES by Mahatma Gandhi (Navjivan) Rs. 1/8, pp. 212.

Gandhiji's writings on rural reconstruction together with reports of certain conversations and articles by a number of co-workers. Also his *Economics of Khadi* (Navjivan) Rs. 4/-, pp. 628, 1941, and *Why the Village Movement?* by Prof. J. C. Kumarappa (Navjivan) Rs. 1/8, for a fuller study of the needs, complexities and solutions of India's rural problem.

GRAMISM by Ram Rai (New Book Co., Bombay) Rs. 10/- pp. 261, 1941.

Gramism—a plea for a New Deal for the peasant masses of India. A thesis on the remaking of Village India, by a writer with 20 years' experience of village work.

REPORT OF THE ROYAL COMMISSION ON INDIAN AGRICULTURE (Govt. of India, Calcutta) pp. 755, 1928.

A comprehensive and painstaking collection of material bearing on Indian agriculture. A very useful summary of the report is also published (Re. 1/-) The volumes of evidence are an inexhaustible mine of information.

---

## FOR FURTHER STUDY

---

For further study the following books will be found of great interest: *Economics of Indian Agriculture* by Prof. B. V. Narayanswami Naidu & P. S. Narasimhan, *Land Problems of India* and *Rural Economy of India*, by Radhakamal Mukherjee, *Agricultural Progress in Western India* by G. Keatinge, *Rural Karnatak* by Dr. M. N. Desai, *Punjab Peasant in Prosperity and Debt*, *Rusticus Loquitur* and *Waste And The Wisdom In The Punjab* all three by Sir Malcolm Darling, *Report of the Floud Commission* (On Permanent Settlement in Bengal), *Tagore on Rural Reconstruction* by Dr. Sudhir Sen, *Socrates in An Indian Village* by F. L. Brayne, *The Problem of Rural Uplift in India* by M. B. Ahmed, *Co-operation and Rural*

*Reconstruction in India* by M. Karamullah Khan, *Landlordism in India* by Dvijadas Dutta, *Peasant Revolts in India* by Indulal Yagnik, *The Indian Farmer, His Wealth and Welfare* by M. G. Bhagat, *Indian Agricultural Statistics* and *Some South Indian Villages* both by Prof. P. J. Thomas, and the *Indian Peasant And His Environment* by Dr. N. Ganguli.

Of a number of valuable economic and social surveys of villages, *Life and Labour in a Deccan Village* by Dr. Harold Mann, and *Survey of Matar Taluka* by Narahari Parikh and J. C. Kumarappa, are notable.

Prof. Brij Narain's valuable studies in Urdu based on research as well as personal investigation, stand in a class by themselves. See his *Punjab-ki-Mali-Halat*, *Zamindaron-ke-Dukhre, Ishtarakiat aur Zamindar, Tansikh-e-Qarzajat,* etc.

Prof. N. G. Ranga's various books call for attention, the more so for his connection with the Peasant Movement here: *Modern Indian Peasant, Kisan Speaks* and *Economic Organisations of Indian Villages* (Taraporewala, Bombay) 2 vols.

## ITALY

LAND RECLAMATION IN ITALY by Cesar Longobard (P. S. King) 12/6, pp. 255, 1936.
Interesting information about Mussolini's efforts to reclaim land, especially near Rome. Pro-Fascist.

## JAPAN

PEASANT UPRISINGS IN JAPAN OF THE TOKUGAWA PERIOD by Dr. Hugh Borton. (Transactions of the Asiatic Society of Japan. Second Series, Vol. XVI, May 1938).

LAND UTILISATION IN JAPAN by S. Nasu (Japanese Council, Inst. of Pacific Relations, Tokyo) 1929.

JAPAN'S FEET OF CLAY by Freda Utley (Faber) 15/-, 1936 (pp. 97 to 159).

## MEXICO

THE MEXICAN AGRARIAN REVOLUTION by P. Tannenbaum (Institute of Economics, New York) $2.50, 1929.

AGRICULTURAL SETTLEMENT IN THE LA LAGUNA REGION, (Ministry of Agriculture, Mexico), pp. 16, 1938.

EJIDO: MEXICO'S WAY OUT by M. E. Simpson (Univ. of North Carolina Pr.) $5, 1937.

The remarkable experiments for the reorganisation of Mexico's land system and rural economy, known as Ejido,—have a great lesson for India. They were initiated, as so many other reforms were, during the time that General Lazaro Cardenas was President of Mexico (1934-1940). Though the results were not everywhere upto expectations, success in the La Laguna Region was very encouraging.

## SOVIET RUSSIA

THE ECONOMICS OF SOVIET AGRICULTURE by L. E. Hubbard (Macmillan) 12/6, pp. 316, 1931.

A comprehensive and scholarly study of Soviet agricultural economy from the origin of serfdom and reforms of Peter the Great to present times. Such topics as the Emancipation of the Serfs (1861), the Peasant Under the Stress of the War of 1914-1918, through the Kerensky and the Bolshevik Revolutions, under the NEP, and Collectivisation of Agriculture, are lucidly dealt with. Also the questions of State exactions, Domestic Economy in Collective Farms, What Collectivisation Has Done For The Peasant, and the Effect of Machinery on Agriculture.

BUILDING COLLECTIVE FARMS by Joseph Stalin (Modern Books) 2/-, pp. 184, 1931.

Articles written from 1929 to 1931 on collectivisation by the head of the Soviet State.

RED BREAD by Maurice Hindus (Cape) 6/-, pp. 348, 1931.

A graphic picture of the Russian peasant caught in the whirl of collectivisation.

THE U.S.S.R. SPEAKS FOR ITSELF, VOL II. (Agriculture & Transport) (Lawrence & Wishart) 2/6, pp. 104, 1941.

Progress in agriculture reviewed by Soviet experts.

THE RUSSIAN PEASANT by Sir John Maynard (Gollancz), 15/-, 1942.

One of the most readable and interesting books on the subject.

## SWEDEN

SWEDEN: THE MIDDLE WAY by Marquis Childs (Yale Univ. Pr.) $2.50, 1936.

The remarkable progress of the co-operative movement in Sweden. How unemployment and poverty have been removed, gross inequalities in wealth graded down and the Middleman between the Producer and the Consumer eliminated with resultant prosperity.

## U. S. A.

FARMERS IN A CHANGING WORLD (Year Book of Agriculture for 1940), (Washington D.C.), $1.50, pp. 1215. 1940.

A mass of information about the conditions of farmers in the U.S.A. as also elsewhere.

GRAPES OF WRATH by John Steinbeck (Various Editions, 2/6 to 8/6) Modern Library, N.Y. 95 cents.

A remarkable novel that depicts the harrowing effects of widespread mechanisation, especially of high tension tractor-farming, on American agriculture, and the life of the farming population.

FARMERS AND WORKERS IN AMERICAN POLITICS by S. A. Rice (Columbia Univ. Pr.)

FARM POLICIES UNDER THE NEW DEAL (Public Affairs Committee, N.Y.), 10 cents. pp. 32, 1942.

AMERICAN AGRICULTURE (1899-1939), by H. Barger and H. H. Laudsberg, 1942.

# THE WOMEN'S MOVEMENT

The story of the evolution of Woman from subjection to comradeship forms one of the most cheering narratives in history. But the fight was by no means an easy one. The question of Woman entering public life and the professions aroused the most acute controversy. The powerful help of satire was often sought to discredit the growing feminist movement. Thus a conservative wit:

> If Women sat in Parliament
> A thing unprecedented—
> The great part of our nation, then,
> Would be Miss-represented.

Fascist ideology launched a new offensive on feminism. Dr. Goebbels, Nazi Minister of Propaganda and Emlightenment declared:

"Politics are for men only—absolutely and unconditionally . . . Women's place is in the family, her proper task is to provide her country and her people with children. It will be Government's duty so to revolutionise the status of women, that she can once again fulfil her most important national function. The liberaion of women is a danger to the State. She must leave to man, the things that belong to man."

## GENERAL

THE EVOLUTION OF WOMAN FROM SUBJECTION TO COMRADESHIP by G. W. Johnson, (Hodden), pp. 276, 1926.

The story of the liberation of woman. The stages, the tactics, the programme.

THE ROAD TO SUCCESS edited by Margaret Cole (Methuen), 7/6, pp. 271, 1936.

Twenty essays on the choice of a career for women with an introduction by the Editor. Among the contributors Ellen Wilkinson writes on *Organising On Political Work;* Daisy Lansbury on *Private Secretary;* Storm Jameson on *The Writer;* Marjorie Cohen on *Social Worker;* Margaret Cole on *Running Two Jobs: Home & Outside Work,* Muriel Potter on *Teaching Profession;* Dr. Winifred Kok on *Medicine.*

WOMEN AND THE REVOLUTION by Ethel Mannin (Secker and Warburg) 7/6, pp. 314, 1938.

Biographical sketches of famous women who have taken a prominent part in different revolutions, written with all the flair and brilliance associated with Ethel Mannin.

SEVEN WOMEN AGAINST THE WORLD by Margaret Goldsmith 10/6, pp. 234.

Seven remarkable figures—Charlotte Corday, Theriogne de Mericourt, Flora Tristan. Louis Michel, Vera Figner, Emma Goldman & Rosa Luxemburg. An analysis of why they revolted against the social system into which they were born and why some of them considered it even worthwhile to pay for their principles with their lives.

A VINDICATION OF THE RIGHTS OF WOMEN by Mary Wollstonecroft (Dent), 3/-, 1792.

Written with all the fervour and indignation of the pioneer. The Everyman's Library edition also includes in the same volume, John Stuart Mill's famous book THE SUBJECTION OF WOMEN (1869).

INTELLIGENT WOMEN'S GUIDE TO SOCIALISM by Bernard Shaw, (Penguin) 2 vols. 9d. each.

A famous book appealing to the Intelligent Woman to accept Socialism.

## CHINA

PORTRAIT OF A CHINESE LADY AND CERTAIN OF HER CONTEMPORARIES by Lady Dorothea Hosie, (Hodder & Stoughton), 7/6.

A study of Chinese woman in all her elegance and subjection.

## ENGLAND

THE CAUSE: A SHORT HISTORY OF THE WOMEN'S MOVEMENT IN GREAT BRITAIN by Ray Strachey (Bell), 15/-, pp. 429, 1928.

A careful and compact description of the Women's Movement from 1792 to 1928. An interesting account of the women's claims and struggle for higher education, the slow opening up of the professions and of the fight for the extension of franchise. Biographical sketches of feminist leaders add to the interest of the book.

## FRANCE

THE POSITION OF WOMEN IN CONTEMPORARY FRANCE by Frances Clark, (P. S. King), 12/6, 1937.

A survey of the French Women in modern society. The author examines the subject from several angles --educational, economic, political, legal and religious.

## GERMANY

WOMEN IN NAZI GERMANY by Katherine Thomas (Gollancz), 3/6, 1943.

A description and an attack on the position of woman in Nazi Germany.

## INDIA

OUR CAUSE Edited by Miss Shyamkumari Nehru (Kitabistan, Allahabad). Rs. 3/-, pp. 419, 1936.

A symposium in which thirty leaders of the Women's Movement collaborate.

Retrospect, Health, Education, The Arts, Industry, Rural Life, Social Evils, Marriage and Divorce, Legal Rights, Political Struggle and the Future of Indian Women, show the large range of subjects treated. Kamaladevi contributes a thought-provoking essay on "The Future of Indian Women's Movement" and Mrs. Uma Nehru on "Whither Women?". Miss Cornelia Sorabji and Lady Wazir Hasan write on the position of Hindu and Muslim women fifty years ago, respectively. The Editor contributes a paper on "Legal Form of Marriage in India."

TO THE WOMEN by Mahatma Gandhi (Pub. Hingorani: Karachi).

A collection of Gandhiji's writings on the subject published over many years.

WOMEN OF INDIA by Oho Rothfield, (Taraporewalla: Bombay) Rs. 20/-, and Rs. 11/-, pp. 222, 1928. 48 Full page colour plates by Dhurandhar.

WOMEN IN MODERN INDIA by Evelyn Gedge & Mithan Choksi (Taraporewalla, Bombay), Reduced to Rs. 3/-, pp. 161, 1929.

INDIAN WOMANHOOD by Mrs. Margaret Cousins (Kitabistan), Rs. 3/-, 1942.

DAUGHTERS OF THE DAWN by G. Venkatachalam, Rs. 1/8.

THE POSITION OF WOMAN by Mrs. Lakshmi N. Menon, (Oxford Pamphlet) Annas Six, 1944.

TO WOMEN by Rajkumari Amrit Kuar, (Navjivan Press, Ahmedabad), Six Annas, 1945.

## JAPAN

THE SOCIAL STATUS OF JAPANESE WOMEN by Waka Yamada (Kokukai Bunka Shinkokai, i.e., Society for International Cultural Relations, Tokyo) Rs. 1/8, pp. 24, 1935. A brief but valuable essay discussing the status and role of women in present-day Japan.

## THE NEAR AND THE MIDDLE EAST

MOSLEM WOMEN ENTER A NEW WORLD by Ruth F. Woodsmall (Allen & Unwin), 12/6, pp. 432, 1936. The book sponsored by the American University of Beirut, attempts a survey of broad tendencies affecting the position of Muslim women in Egypt, Palestine, Syria, Transjordan, Turkey, Iraq, Persia and India. Examines the Purdah System, Early Marriage, Polygamy, Divorce, Education, Economic Opportunity in

Professional and Commercial Life, Health, Political Aspirations and Religious Attitudes. There are 31 full page illustrations.

THE MOSLEM WORLD TO-DAY Edited by John R. Mott (Hodder & Stoughton), 10/6, pp. 420, 1925. Three chapters —14th, 15th and 16th are devoted to women.

## SOVIET RUSSIA

WOMEN IN SOVIET RUSSIA by Fanina Halle (Routledge), 8/6, pp. 409, 1935, and WOMEN IN THE SOVIET EAST by Fanina Halle (Secker & Warburg), 15/-, pp. 363, 1938. Illustrations.
Discuss every aspect of women's work in a sympathetic spirit.

THE POSITION OF WOMEN IN THE U.S.S.R. by G. N. Serebrennikov (Gollancz), 7/6, pp. 288, 1937.
A statement of the aims of Soviet legislation affecting the position of women as also a careful examination of the extent to which these aims have been realised.

## TURKEY

TURKISH WOMAN IN HISTORY, Issued by the Press Department of the Ministry of the Interior, Ankara. pp. 33, 1937.
The story of the remarkable emancipation of woman, and of her part in the making of the new Turkey.

## U. S. A.

JANE ADDAMS: A BIOGRAPHY by James Weber Linn (Appleton-Century) 15/-, pp. 457, 1935.
The authoritative life of Jane Addams, social worker, founder of the Hull House, Nobel Prize-woman, one of the greatest figures of modern America, by her nephew.

# THE YOUTH MOVEMENT

The literature on the Youth Movement lies buried largely in the files of Journals, scores of them, printed in all countries of the world. The number of books on the Youth Movement is surprisingly small. The following represents a selection of the more important ones among them.

It is as well to notice that the Youth Movement today is not an integrated phenomenon. It has so many different aspects. The international aspect was getting to be the most important, especially after the First World War of 1914-18. The idea that the youth of all countries should unite in one great international movement, to put an end to War and to usher in a new social order, for a time seemed to have gripped the mind of the post-war generation in Europe. A number of important International Youth Conferences helped to strengthen this view. The rise of Fascism, however, gave a set back to this tendency. Mussolini first, and then Hitler, realising the tremendous significance of the Youth Movement became its ardent protagonists in their own countries and gave it a "nationalist" orientation.

"Catch Them Young" became a universally popular slogan with governments of the leading countries, most of whom started youth organisations under state auspices. Their activities include types of physical education, military training, facilities for travel, etc.

## ENGLAND

YOUTH ORGANISATIONS OF GREAT BRITAIN, Edited by Douglas Cook (Jarrolds) 8/6, 1944.

A comprehensive survey of youth work in Britain.

IN THE SERVICE OF YOUTH by Dr. Josephine Brew, (Faber), 7/6, 1943.

A practical manual of work among adolescents.

YOUTH HOSTELS HANDBOOK (Welwyn Garden City) 8d., pp. 48, 1942.

A useful little manual full of interesting information published by the Youth Hostels Association, London.

YOUNG MINDS FOR OLD Edited by Lincoln Ralphs, (Muller) 5/-, 1936.

A series of 14 articles written by students representing all the leading British Universities. The contributors write from widely differing points of view—Socialist, Communist, Christian, Liberal, and even "non-political". They discuss different problems that concern the students as well as broader national and international questions, whose pressure is now being felt even in the academic atmosphere of Universities. Mr. Reginald Smith writes about "Socialist Movement in the Universities".

## CHINA

PRELUDE TO WAR: THE CHINESE STUDENT REBELLION of 1935-36 by Hubert Freyne (China Journal Publishing Co., Shanghai), pp. 122, 1939, Illustrated.

Vividly describes student life in China. Also their activities in town and countryside to rouse the people.

YOUTH MOVEMENT IN CHINA by T. C. Wang (New Republic, N.Y.), $1.00, 1926.

The Chinese Youth Movement, in its various aspects, with special stress on the part of the foreign-returned students have played in the building of Chinese national movement. Attractive and readable.

## GERMANY

YOUTH WELFARE IN GERMANY by J. W. Taylor (Baird-Ward Co., Tennesse, U.S.A.), $3.75, pp. 259, 1936.

A valuable study of German Youth Movement, covering the last quarter of a century, with particular emphasis on the activities of the Hitler Youth. Some of the chapters are: Historical Development of the German Youth Welfare Agencies; Their Organisation, Support and Activities; Physical Training, Propaganda; Press and Film; Radio; Youth Hostels; Leadership, Country Homes for City Schools, Youth Libraries, Youth and Unemployment, Youth Politics. Home and School, Broader Implications of the Youth Welfare Activities. In the appendix are given translations of 14 laws affecting Youth, including relevant sections from the National Youth Welfare Act.

HITLER YOUTH by Hans Siemson (Lindsay Drummond), Paper, 3/6, pp. 279, 1943.

"This is a fascinating book and a terrifying one. For it gives a true picture of modern German youth. This is what we are up against." (Peter Nathan: "Psychology of Fascism", p. 152).

EDUCATION FOR DEATH by Grigor Zeimer (Constable), 7/6, pp. 196, 1942.

A remarkable study of the German Youth Movement and the part that the Educational system plays in weaning youth to the policies of the Nazi State. The book has been filmed under the title "Hitler's Children."

## INDIA

YOUTH MOVEMENT IN THE BOMBAY PRESIDENCY by Yusuf Meherally (Bombay Presidency Youth League, Bombay), pp. 20, 1928.

A brief account of the rise and the growth of the Youth Movement in the Bombay Presidency.

THE STUDENT MOVEMENT IN INDIA by Prabodh Chandra (Lahore) Rs. 2/-, pp. 160, 1938.

A survey that tends to be rather over-enthusiastic, written by one of the prominent leaders of the Students' Movement in India.

TO THE STUDENTS by Mahatma Gandhi, (Pub. by Hingorian: Karachi).
Gandhiji's writings on the subject, collected together for convenient reference.

## ITALY

THE OPERA NAZIONALE BALILLA (Palazzo Viminale, Rome), pp. 105, 1927. With many illustrations.
Excellently produced Fascist brochure which shows that "the Fascist Revolution, like all great movements which have left an indelible trace upon social order, has as a fundamental necessity, placed at its base the problem of the training of youth. The "Opera Nazionale Balilla" has been purposely created to solve this complex and delicate problem upon the solution of which undoubtedly rests the continuation of the historic function of Fascism throughout all time."
Youth Organisations were created by the Law of April 3, 1926. Its membership is restricted to children between the age of 8 to 14. While the *Avanguardisti* ranged in age from 14 to 18.

## NEAR AND MIDDLE EAST

YOUNG ISLAM ON TREK by Basil Mathews (H.O.P., Edinburgh), 2/-, pp. 208.
A very readable description of the Youth Movement in the countries of the Near and the Middle East, including Turkey. It shows the impact of new thought and technique upon the youth of these countries.

FERMENT IN THE YOUTH OF ISLAM by Basil Mathews.
Being Chapter V in THE MOSLEM WORLD TODAY (pp. 61-78), Edited by John R. Mott. (Hodder & Stoughton), 10/6, pp. 420, 1925.

## SOVIET RUSSIA

YOUTH IN SOVIET RUSSIA by Klaus Mehnert (Allen & Unwin), 7/6, pp. 270, 1933.

There are, says the writer, more than 100 million people under 25 in the Soviet Union. He proceeds to give an interesting description of the Student life, Youth Communes, Komsomols, Literature of Youth in Russia of To-day, etc.

THE YOUTH OF RUSSIA TO-DAY by H. Spaull (Ivor Nicholson & Watson), 3/6, pp. 168, 1933.

A description of Youth Movement in Russia and the efforts launched to organise their leisure and to build up their lives according to the plan of the State.

## U. S. A.

ORGANISATION FOR YOUTH by E. R. Pendry & Hugh Hartshorne (McGraw-Hill) 15/-, pp. 359, 1935.

A useful handbook giving a succinct account of 40 leading American Youth Associations; prepared after exhausting investigation. Special stress is laid on leisure time activities. Some of the associations described are: Pioneer Youth of America; Woodcraft League of America; Boys' Brotherhood Republic; Junior Achievement; Pathfinders of America; Campfire Girls; Y.M.C.A.; Y.W.C.A.; Boy Scouts; Toc H. etc. "In connection with each organisation is a statement of its main purpose, its history and growth, its programme and procedure, its philosophy and method, its use of motives and awards and such evidence of its success, as its proponents cared to offer." (viii).

# CO-OPERATIVE MOVEMENT

The Co-operative Movement celebrated the centenary of its birth on December 21, 1944. A hundred years from that date, the Rochdale Pioneers—28 poor weavers of Rochdale, Lancashire, England with a capital of £28 (subscribed in small weekly instalments) founded the first co-operative union. From this very modest beginning, the movement has grown to impressive proportions. Today nearly half of all families in Great Britain belong to it. (Nine million members from five million families). In 1943, it had a turnover of £202,000,000 and produced in factories owned by itself things worth £61,600,000. The Co-operatives controls 10 per cent of England's retail trade and 12 per cent of all her food. It is backed by its own bank, insurance society, steamships and employs over 300,000 persons. "Shop at the Co-op." has been an increasingly popular slogan.

The most spectaculalr developments have, however been in the Scandinavian countries especially Sweden and Denmark. It has helped their Socialist Governments largely to abolish poverty, unemployment and glaring inequality in wealth and strengthen the democratic way of life.

In India, its progress under foreign rule has been disappointing. But the future remains.

The International Co-operative Alliance was formed in 1895. In it are associated the leading National Co-operative Movements of the world. At the outbreak of the World War II in 1939, 141 National Unions and Federations with an aggregate membership of 72 millions, representing 35 countries were associated with it.

## GENERAL

WORLD CO-OPERATION, 1844-1944 by Dr. N. Barou (Fabian Publications) 2/-, pp. 52, 1944.
A brief but highly informative account of the rise of the Co-operative Movement during the first hundred years of its life.

CO-OPERATION AT HOME AND ABROAD by Prof. C. R. Fay (P. S. King) 15/- pp. 480, 1920. (Latest edition 1936.)
A standard book, valuable alike for a description and analysis of the Co-operative Movement in Great Britain and the Continent of Europe.

HOW TO TELL PROGRESS FROM REACTION by Manya Gordon (E. P. Dutton) $3 pp. 320, 1944.
A most stimulating study, in which the author sees in the Co-operative Movement the process, by which humanity is civilising itself and marching on to socialism.

CO-OPERATIVE SOCIETIES THROUGHOUT THE WORLD (International Labour Office: Geneva), 1939.
Important Numerical Data.

CO-OPERATIVE ORGANISATIONS AND POST-WAR RELIEF, (International Labour Office: Montreal), 4/-, pp. 173, 1943.
A documentary study. A discussion of its working, both in the urban and rural fields. Also an assessment of its role in the solution of problems created by the War.

YEAR BOOK OF AGRICULTURAL CO-OPERATION Edited by the Horace Plunkett Foundation, London and published by the Co-operative Wholesale Society, Manchester.
A most valuable reference book.

PEOPLE'S YEAR BOOK, (C.W.S. Manchester) (see section: REFERENCE Books).

## CHINA

CHINA BUILDS FOR DEMOCRACY by Nym Wales (Kitabistan, Allahabad), Rs. 5/4, pp.
The remarkable story of the Chinese Industrial Co-operatives.

## FRANCE—GERMANY—ITALY

CO-OPERATION AT HOME AND ABROAD by C. R. Fay, (P. S. King), 15/-, pp. 480, 1920. Revised 1936.
Specially for an interesting account of the Co-operatives in the pre-Nazi Germany. The Nazis were not keen on the Movement and both Germany and Italy withdrew from the International Co-operative Alliance.

## GREAT BRITAIN

CO-OPERATION by F. Hall (Principal of the Co-operative College (Manchester) and W. P. Watkins (C.W. S. Manchester) 7/6 pp. 408, 1937.
A survey of the history, principles and organisation of the Co-operative Movement in Great Britain and Ireland.

THE ENGLISH CO-OPERATIVES by S. R. Elliot (Yale Univ. Press) $3, pp. 212, 1937.
An extremely well written account by an English expert.

## INDIA

CO-OPERATIVE MOVEMENT IN INDIA by Dr. E. M. Hough (P. S. King) 15/- 1932.
Well-written but out of date. Excellent Bibliography.

ORIGIN AND GROWTH OF CO-OPERATION IN INDIA by Vaikunth L. Mehta (1928).

A very able and painstaking account, by undoubtedly the greatest authority on the Co-operative Movement in India.

REVIEW OF THE CO-OPERATIVE MOVEMENT IN INDIA, (Pub. by the Reserve Bank of India), Bombay 1941.

A highly informative and competent review.

YEAR BOOK AND DIRECTORY OF INDIAN CO-OPERATION, Edited by V. Ramdas Pantalu Rs. 5/- pp. 700, 1942.

A detailed survey, province by province. Very useful.

## JAPAN

THE CO-OPERATIVE MOVEMENT IN JAPAN by Prof. Kiyoshi Ogata of Tokyo University. (P. S. King), 12/6, pp. 378.

A scholarly survey. Preface by Sidney Webb.

## DENMARK

Coward MC Cann $2.50, pp. 293, 1936. A picture of pre-war Denmark as a Co-operative Paradise.

CO-OPERATIVE WAY by F. C. Howe.

## SWEDEN

CO-OPERATION IN SWEDEN by Axel Jgores (C. W. S. Manchester) 1937.

A heartening account of accomplishment.

SWEDEN: THE MIDDLE WAY by Marquis W. Childs. (Yale Univ. Pr.) $2·50, 1936. Details the remarkable progress of the Co-operative Movement in Sweden, including the abolition of poverty and unemployment.

## SOVIET UNION

CO-OPERATION IN THE U.S.S.R. by L. A. Paul. (Gollancz) 3/6, pp. 160, 1934.

A favourable account of the Consumer's movement.

SOVIET AGRICULTURAL CO-OPERATION by Dr. N. Barou 1943.

A paper read at a conference in London, organised by the British Association for the Advancement of Science on April 16-17, 1943 on "Co-operative Systems in European Agriculture."

## U.S.A. AND THE AMERICAS

CONSUMERS CO-OPERATION IN AMERICA by B. B. Fowler (Vanguard Press N.Y.) $2 pp. 305. 1936.

A lucid and readable account of the aims and achievements of Consumers co-operation in the United States. A story of striking progress in recent years.

THE CO-OPERATIVE MOVEMENT IN THE AMERICAS by M. M. Coady (International Labour Office, Montreal), 1943.

A distinguished educationist records the progress made and the tremendous difficulties in the way.

# OTHER SUBJECTS

No study of the modern world could be regarded as satisfactory without an acquaintance at any rate, with the elements of political and social sciences. The following books, in addition to those already included, each a recognised study, open out fascinating vistas of knowledge and may strongly be recommended.

## POLITICAL SCIENCE

AN INTRODUCTION TO POLITICS by H. J. Laski, (Allen & Unwin), 2/6, pp. 112, 1931. Several Reprints.

A GRAMMAR OF POLITICS by H. J. Laski (Allen & Unwin), 12/6, pp. 672, 1925. Several Reprints since.

HISTORY OF POLITICAL THOUGHT by R. G. Gettel (Allen & Unwin) 15/-, pp. 511, 1924. Many Reprints since.

STORY OF THE POLITICAL PHILOSOPHERS by G. Catlin (McGraw-Hill) 15/-, pp. 802, 1939.

TO THE FINLAND STATION: A STUDY IN THE WRITING AND ACTING OF HISTORY by Edmund Wilson (Secker & Warburg) 20/-, pp. 509, 1940

DECLINE OF THE WEST by Oswald Spengler (Allen & Unwin) 21/-, 1928.

SOCIAL-ECONOMIC MOVEMENTS by H. W. Laidler (Crowell) $5, 1944.

END OF ECONOMIC MAN by Peter Drucker (Heinemann) 7/6, pp. 251, 1939.

FUTURE OF INDUSTRIAL MAN by Peter Drucker (Heinemann) 10/6, pp. 205, 1943.

THE ANATOMY OF REVOLUTION by Crane Brinton (Allen & Unwin) 12/6, pp. 326, 1939.

REVOLUTION FROM 1789 to 1906 by R. W. Postgate, 18/-, 1920. (Plebs. League Ed. 8/6) (Documents).

FREEDOM *vs.* ORGANISATION (1814-1914) by Bertrand Russell, (Allen & Unwin), 8/6, pp. 510, 1934.

## ECONOMICS

OUTLINE OF ECONOMICS (Plebs League) 3/6.

OUTLINE OF ECONOMICS by Lepidus & Ostrovityanov (Martin Lawrence), 12/6.

PRINCIPLES OF ECONOMICS by F. W. Taussig (Macmillan), 2 Vols., 30/-, pp. 547 and 595. Latest Reprint 1943.

PRINCIPLES OF ECONOMICS by E. R. A. Seligman.

MAN'S WORLDLY GOODS by Leo Huberman, (Gollancz), 10/6.

CAMBRIDGE ECONOMIC HANDBOOKS (Several Volumes).

HISTORY OF ECONOMIC DOCTRINES by C. Gide & C. Rist (Harrap), 12/6, pp. 672, 1915. Several Reprints since.

HISTORY OF ECONOMIC THOUGHT by Prof. L. H. Haney (Macmillan) 20/-, pp. 827, 1936.

INDIAN ECONOMICS by Jathar and Beri, (Oxford), 2 vols. Rs. 11/-.

## SOCIOLOGY

SOCIOLOGY by Morris Ginsberg (Home Univ. Library) 3/6, pp. 255, 1934, 2nd. Imp., 1939.

SOCIETY: A TEXT BOOK OF SOCIOLOGY by R. M. MacIver (Macmillan) 18/-, 1931 (Reprinted).

MAKING OF SOCIETY Edited by V. F. Calverton, (Modern Library), 95 cents, pp. 923, 1927.

MODERN SOCIOLOGICAL THEORIES by Pitrim A. Sorokin (Harvard Univ.) $5.

A HISTORY OF SOCIAL DEVELOPMENT by Muller Lyer (Allen & Unwin) 10/6, pp. 362, 1927.

**TECHNICS AND CIVILISATION** by Lewis Mumford (Routledge) 21/-, pp. 495, 1934.

**CULTURE OF CITIES** by Lewis Mumford (Secker & Warburg) 15/-, pp. 542, 1938. Reprinted 1944.

**CONDITION OF MAN** by Lewis Mumford (Secker & Warburg) 25/-, 1944.

**MODERN MAN IN THE MAKING** by Otto Neurath 16/-, 1939.

**THE FEAR OF FREEDOM** by Erich Fromm (Kegan Paul) 15/-, pp. 247, 1942.

**POWER** by Bertrand Russell (Allen & Unwin) 7/6, pp. 328, 1938.

**MAN AND SOCIETY IN AN AGE OF RECONSTRUCTION** by Karl Mannheim (Kegan Paul) 15/-

**RAPE OF THE MASSES** by Serge Chakotin (Chatto & Windus) 7/6.

## ANTHROPOLOGY

**ANTHROPOLOGY** by R. R. Marret (Home Univ. Library) 3/-.

**THE GOLDEN BOUGH** by Sir James Frazer (One Vol. Ed.).

**FOLKWAYS** by William Sumner (Various Editions).

**MAKING OF MAN** Edited by V. F. Calverton (Modern Library) 95 Cents.

**THE MYTH OF THE MIND** by Winwoode Reade (Thinkers Library) 1/3.

**EPICS, MYTHS AND LEGENDS OF INDIA** by P. Thomas (Taraporewala: Bombay) Rs. 19/-. 2nd Ed., 1945. 247 illustrations.

**MYTHS OF THE HINDUS AND BUDDHISTS** by Sister Nivedita and Dr. A. K. Coomarswamy, (Harrap), 10/6, 1913 and 1932. Gorgeous Illustrations.

## PHILOSOPHY

**STORY OF PHILOSOPHY** by Will Durant (Garden City Pub. Co.), $1, Several Ed.

MANSIONS OF PHILOSOPHY by Will Durant (Garden City Pub. Co.) $1, pp. 704, 1929.

A GUIDE TO MODERN THOUGHT by C. E. M. Joad (Faber) 7/6, pp. 255, 1933, Several Reprints.

OUTLINE OF PHILOSOPHY by Bertrand Russell (Allen & Unwin) 12/6.

INDIAN PHILOSOPHY by Sir S. Radhakrishnan, 2 vols. (Allen & Unwin) 21/-. 1929.

ENDS AND MEANS by Aldous Huxley (Chatto & Windus) 5/-, pp. 337, 1937. Several Reprints.

A. B. C. OF PSYCHOLOGY by C. K. Ogden (Penguin) 9d., pp. 144, 1944.

PSYCHOLOGY by William McDouggall (Home Univ. Library), 3/6.

TOTEM AND TABOO by Sigmund Freud (Pelicans) 9d.

PSYCHO-PATHOLOGY OF EVERYDAY LIFE by Sigmund Freud (Pelicans) 9d.

PSYCHO-ANALYSIS AND ITS DERIVATIVES by H. Crichton-Miller (Home Univ. Library) 3/6, pp. 256, 1933, Reprint 1937.

## SCIENCE

SCIENCE FOR THE CITIZEN by Lancelot Hogben (Allen & Unwin) 7/6, pp. 285, 1941.

MATHEMATICS FOR THE MILLION by Lancelot Hogben (Allen & Unwin) 12/6, pp. 686, 1936, 15th, Imp., 1943.

THE SCIENTIFIC OUTLOOK by Bertrand Russell (Allen & Unwin) 7/6, pp. 285, 1931.

THE MYSTERIOUS UNIVERSE by Sir James Jeans (Penguins) 9d.

THE EXPANDING UNIVERSE by Sir Arthur Eddington (Pelicans) 9d.

## ART

THE ARTS OF MANKIND by Hendrik Van Loon, (Harrap), 15/-, pp. 571, 1938.

HISTORY OF ART by Eli Faure (Garden City Pub. Co.) Five Vols., $1.98 each.

A SHORT HISTORY OF ART by A. Blum & R. R. Totleck (Scribners) $7.50. pp. 291. 1926.

THE MEANING OF ART by Herbert Read (Faber) 6/-, pp. 224, 1931, Reprint 1943.

HISTORY OF INDIAN AND INDONESIAN ART by A. K. Coomarswamy (E. Goldstein), 50/-, pp. 295, 1927. Numerous Plates.

A HANDBOOK OF INDIAN ART by E. B. Havell (Murray) 25/-, pp. 222, 1920, Several Plates.

## MISCELLANEOUS

STORY OF THE WORLD'S LITERATURE by John Macy (Garden City Pub. Co.) De Luxe Ed. $1.98, pp. 613, 1925, Revised 1936, Illustrated.

CRY FOR JUSTICE: An Anthology of the Literature of Social Protest, Edited by Upton Sinclair $1.25.

PRISON ANTHOLOGY Edited by Reginald Reynolds & Dinah Stock.

THE BIBLE OF THE WORLD (Scriptures of Eight Principal Religions) Edited by R. O. Ballou, 25/-. (The American edition called *The Pocket World Bible* is priced at $2.50, Viking Pr.)

ON RELIGION by Lenin (Various Cheap Ed.)

RELIGION AND SCIENCE by Bertrand Russell (Home Univ. Library) 3/-.

THE MARTYRDOM OF MAN by Winwoode Reade (Thinkers Library) 1/3.

RELIGION AND THE RISE OF CAPITALISM by R. H. Tawney (Penguins) 9d.

THE YOGI AND THE COMMISSAR by Arthur Koestler (Cape) 10/6, 1945.

# REFERENCE BOOKS

PENGUIN POLITICAL DICTIONARY compiled by Walter Theimer, (Penguin Books) 9d. pp. 255.
A marvel of compressed information.

PENGUIN POLITICAL ATLAS, Edited by S. C. Johnson, (Penguin Books) 9d.

THE STATESMAN'S YEAR BOOK Edited by M. Epstein (Macmillan) 30/-.
A statistical and historical annual of the States of the world. Handy, useful and complete.

THE POLITICAL HANDBOOK OF THE WORLD Edited by W. H. Mallory (Published for the Council on Foreign Relations, New York) (Harper) $2.50, pp. 208.
Contains up-to-date information about the composition of Parliaments, the programmes and leaders of parties and the trend of the newspapers of all the countries of the world.

SURVEY ON INTERNATIONAL AFFAIRS Edited by A. J. Toynbee & V. M. Boulter (Oxford).
An annual publication indispensable for students of international affairs for reference. Hitherto several volumes have been published in the series, the first being for 1920-1923. Subsequently one or more volumes have been published each year.

DOCUMENTS ON INTERNATIONAL AFFAIRS Edited by J. W. Wheeler-Bennet & Stephen Heald (Oxford).
An invaluable source book for the student of International affairs.

ECONOMIST'S YEAR BOOK Edited by G. Verwey & D. C. Renooji (Simpkin, London).

A manual of Statistical sources.

**THE PEOPLE'S YEAR BOOK** (Co-operative Workers' Society Publicity Dept., Manchester) Popular Edition 1/- (Cloth 3/-).

A useful reference book for Trade Unionists, Co-operators and students. Articles on Co-operative Movement, Trade Union Movement, Literature, Legislative events of the year, Facts and Figures about Industry, Finance, Employment, Wages, Social Conditions, etc.

**WHO'S WHO: AN ANNUAL BIOGRAPHICAL DICTIONARY** (A. & C. Black), 70/-, pp. 3730.
Contains approximately 40,000 names.

**WHO WAS WHO:** (1897-1915) 21/-, (1916-1928) 21/-, (1929-1940) 40/-, pp. 1500. (All A. & C. Black).

**WRITERS' AND ARTISTS' YEAR BOOK** (A. & C. Black) 5/-.

Contains an up-to-date list of journals and magazines, their addresses, requirements and scales of payment; information containing British and American publishers, advice to writers, essential details regarding copyright, agreements, dramatic and serial rights.

**THE OXFORD DICTIONARY OF QUOTATIONS** (Oxford Univ. Press) 25/-, pp. 879, 1941.

One of the most famous and one of the most enjoyable reference books in the English language. Gives 40,000 familiar quotations. Index consists of 302 pages.

**CRY FOR JUSTICE**: An Anthology of the Literature of Social Protest Edited by Upton Sinclair, (Pub. Upton Sinclair, California, U.S.A.) $1.25, pp. 891, 1921. Illustrated.

Writings of Philosophers, Poets, Novelists and others who have voiced the struggle against social injustice. Selected from 25 languages, covering a period of 5000 years.

## YEAR BOOKS

Several important year books are published annually, like the China Year Book, Japan Year Book, French Year Book, Near East Year Book, Year Book of the League of Nations, I.L.O. Year Book, Year Book of Labour Statistics, Armaments Year Book, Municipal Year Book etc., giving useful and authoritative information on their respective countries or subjects. The war has interfered with the regular publication of some of these.

---

## SOME REFERENCE BOOKS ON INDIA

---

THE INDIAN ANNUAL REGISTER Editor: Nripendranath Mitra (The Annual Register Office, Calcutta) Issued in two six monthly volumes. Subscription Rs. 14/- per year. An annual digest of the Public Affairs of India. A comprehensive and reliable record of almost every phase of national life and activity: political, economic, social, educational, etc. Published since 1919. Invaluable to every student of Public Affairs in India.

INDIAN YEAR BOOK AND WHO'S WHO, Edited by Sir Francis Low. ('Times of India' Press, Bombay), Rs. 10/-, pp. 1500.

An important book of reference. Packed with useful information, which generally has a pro-British, bias.

HINDUSTAN YEAR BOOK (M. C. Sarkar, Calcutta), Rs. 2/4.

NALANDA YEAR BOOK (Calcutta) Rs. 2/8.

NEW YEAR BOOK (Calcutta) Rs. 2/-.

Three very necessary handbooks, giving information on various topics mainly concerning India. Extremely good value, for the price.

INDIAN WHO'S WHO, Edited by Waman P. Kapadi (Yeshanand & Co., Bombay), Rs. 10/-, 1937.

Contains biographical sketches of all important persons in India. A valuable reference book.

INDIAN FINANCE YEAR BOOK ('Indian Finance' Office, Calcutta).

A source book of commercial and trade statistics.

STATISTICAL ABSTRACT FOR BRITISH INDIA (Govt. of India, Calcutta).

Issued for decennial periods from 1840 to date. Deals with area and population, justice, police and prisons, municipalities, shipping, trade, coinage, railways, foreign trade, post office, army, education, public works, factories, industrial census, agriculture and land tenure, etc. Contains statistics about a number of Indian States also.

---

# ADDITIONAL NAMES

---

Some very new books, others on countries in the world's headlines, since the end of World War II are noted here.

## INDIA

RECENT POLITICAL DEVELOPMENTS (See p. 18)

JAI HIND (Janmabhoomi Press: Bombay) Rs. 5/- 1945. The story of the Indian National Army. Illustrations.

THE COMMERCIAL PROBLEM (pp. 20-21)

A GUIDE TO THE COMMUNAL PROBLEM IN INDIA by Babu Anugrah Narayan Singh (Himalaya Publications: Patna) Rs. 5/- pp. 309, 1945.

THE MUSLIM LEAGUE by W. Cantwell Smith (Minerva Bookshop: Lahore) Rs. 2/-. 1945.

### PLANNING (p. 24)

PICTURE OF A PLAN by M. R. Masani (Oxford) Rs. 2/-. 1945.

Brilliantly written and illustrated. An exquisite example of book printing.

POVERTY AND SOCIAL CHANGE by Tarlok Singh, (Longmans), Rs. 3/8, 1945.

### BIOGRAPHICAL NOTE (pp. 30 to 33)

*Life and Times of Sir Phirozeshah Mehta* by the Rt. Hon. Srinivasa Sastry, *Eminent Bihar Contemporaries* by Dr. Sachidananda Sinha and *Aurobindo Ghosh* by Prof. K. R. Srinivasa Iyengar are welcome additions. Among earlier books consult: *Ranade* by D. G. Karve, *Gokhale* by J. S. Hoyland, *Mahatma Gandhi* by R. M. Gray and Manilal Parekh.

### OF LITERARY INTEREST (pp. 31 to 33)

Three well known novels, all in recent English translations are: *Malancha* (The Flower Garden) by Rabindranath Tagore, splendidly translated by Krishna Kripalani (*Hindustan Standard* Puja Number 1945, Calcutta) *Srikant* by Sarat Chandra Chatterji, considered by many to be his masterpiece (trans. by K. Sen) and *Epoch's End* by Tarashankar Bannerji (trans. by H. N. Mukherji).

A revealing book on the famous writer, Munshi Premchand in Hindi, by his wife, Shivrani Devi, entitled *Premchand Ghar Me*, is of great interest. *Iqbal* by Roop Krishna, well known artist and critic is a sparkling essay, beautifully printed.

## THE FAR EAST

### BURMA (p. 44)

THE STORY OF BURMA by Tennyson Jesse (Macmillan) 12/6, 1945.

The most comprehensive recent book on Burma.

### "DUTCH" EAST INDIES (INDONESIA) (p. 45)

For a study of the background of the revolt in Indonesia, *The Dutch East Indies* by A. Vandenbosch (1941) and *Netherlands India* by J. S. Furnival (1939) will be found useful. For economic conditions consult *The Structure of Netherlands Indian Economy* by J. H. Boeke (1942) and *The Economic Development of the Netherlands Indies* by J. O. M. Broek (1942). Among other recent books of interest *Netherlands Indies and Japan* by Dr. H. J. Van Mook (1944) and *Javanese Panorama* by H. W. Ponder (1942) deserve attention. A truly beautiful book is *The Island of Bali* by M. Covarrubias, famous Mexican artist, packed full of illustrations. *The Ageless Indies* by R. Kennedy (1942) is also good. For the influence of Indian culture, see *Hindu Colonies in the Far East* by Dr. R. C. Muzumdar and *India And The Pacific* by Dr. Kalidas Nag.

## "FRENCH" INDO-CHINA (p. 45)

Likewise *French Indo-China* by Virginia Thompson (1937) *Little China: The Annamese Land of Indo-China* by B. H. Broderick (1942) and *The French Policy and Development in Indo-China* by T. E. Ennis (1936) and *The French Colonies* by Jules Stein (1944) provide the background to the rebellion in Indo-China. *The Economic Development of French Indo-China* by C. Robequain (1945) and *Labour Conditions in Indo-China* (International Labour Office, Geneva) (1938) give the economic facts. For the influence of Indian culture see Kalidas Nag's *India and the Pacific* and R. C. Muzumdar's *Hindu Colonies in the Far East*. *Angkor the Magnificent* by H. C. Candee (1925) and *Cambodian Glory* by H. W. Ponder (1936) are valuable accounts of past greatness.

## MANCHURIA & MONGOLIA (CHINA) (pp. 37 & 45)

*Manchukuo: Jewel of Asia* by D. M. B. Collier and C. Lestrange Malone (1936) and *International Rivalries in Manchuria* (1689-1922) by P. H. Clyde (1922) may be consulted.

*The New Mongolia* by L. Forbath (1936) *The Forbidden Journey: From Peking to Kashmir* by Ella Maillert (1937) *Travels In Tartary* by Peter Fleming (1934-

36) and *Russia, Japan and Mongolia* by G. D. R. Phillips (1942) are of interest.

## THE ARAB WORLD (pp. 48 and 50)

EAST IS WEST by Freya Stark, Murray) 12/6 1945. Experiences of a well known writer in Arabia, Egypt, Palestine, Syria, Iraq and Iran.

SYRIA AND LEBANON by A. H. Hourani (Royal Institute of International Affairs) 18/- 1945.

IN THE HIGH YEMEN by H. Scott (1942).

## AFGHANISTAN (p. 52)

TRAVELS IN AFGHANISTAN 1937-38 by E. F. Fox (Macmillan) $4, pp. 285, 1943. (appreciative).

## SWITZERLAND (p. 86)

THE GOVERNMENT OF SWITZERLAND by W. E. Rappard (1937).

## U. S. A. (pp. 93-94)

12 MILLION BLACK VOICES by Richard Wright & E. Rosskam (Viking Press. N.Y.) $3, pp. 152, 1941. 147 photographs. (Splendid).

## AFRICA (p. 102)

THE GOVERNMENT OF FRENCH NORTH AFRICA by H. J. Liebesny (Lippincott: Philadelphia) 1943.

PRESENT DAY MOROCCO by O. H. Warne (1937).

ANGLO-EGYPTIAN SUDAN FROM WITHIN. Edited by J. A. de C. Hamilton (1937).

THE AFRICAN TRILOGY by Alan Moorhead (1945) the well known correspondent's three war books in one volume.

## SOCIALISM (pp. 104 to 112)

THE SOCIALIST TRADITION by Prof. Alexander Gray (Longmans) 21/- 1945.

A History of Socialist Ideas from the earliest times of the present day.

DEMOCRACY AND SOCIALISM by Arthur Rosenberg (Bell) 12/6, pp. 363, 1939.

LIFE AND TEACHINGS OF ENGELS by Z. K. Coates (Lawrence and Wishart) 6/-, 1945.

CAPITAL by Karl Marx, 3 vols. (Saraswati Press, Calcutta) Rs. 42. (1944-45).

MEMOIRS OF A REVOLUTIONIST by P. Kropotkin (several editions).

TOWARDS CHRISTIAN DEMOCRACY by Sir Stafford Cripps (Allen and Unwin) 5/-, 1945.

WHAT IS SINGLE TAX by Louis F. Post (Vanguard Press) 1926.

HENRY GEORGE by A. J. Nock (Morrow, N.Y.) 1939.

## CAPITALISM (pp. 117-8-9)

DYNAMIC CAPITALISM by C. W. Hazelett (Harper) 1943.

BUSINESS AS A SYSTEM OF POWER by Robert A. Brady Columbia Univ. Press, $4, 1943.

POLITICAL ECONOMY AND CAPITALISM by Maurice Dobb (Routledge) 12/6, 1937.

THE NATURE OF CAPITALIST CRISIS by John Strachey (Gollancz) 5/- 1935.

PRIVATE MONOPOLY by David Lasser (Harper) $3, 1945.

## LABOUR MOVEMENT (pp. 136 & 142)

INTERNATIONAL LABOUR MOVEMENT by John Price (Royal Institute of International Affairs) 15/- 1945.

A SHORT HISTORY OF LABOUR CONDITIONS IN GERMANY (1800-1932) by J. Kuczynski (Muller) 8/6, 1945.

## CO-OPERATIVE MOVEMENT (p. 167)

CO-OPERATION IN THE COLONIES (Fabian Colonial Bureau) 7/6, 1945.